FORTUNE-TEL

M000284306

The first practical manual of divination using the ancient
Chinese game of Mah Jongg.

龜筮協從圖

帝舜

大禹

諸臣

Frontispiece: Divination by tortoise carapace and milfoil. The Emperor (left background) and his ministers look on anxiously as the two magicians (left foreground) prepare the tortoise carapace and the milfoil (yarrow) stalks for divination. The two Chinese characters 占 and 卜 are pictorial representations of these ancient instruments (see p. 20).

FORTUNE~TELLING BY MAH JONGG

A Practical Guide to Divination Using the Ancient Chinese Game of Mah Jongg

by

DEREK WALTERS

THE AQUARIAN PRESS
Wellingborough, Northamptonshire

First published as Your Future Revealed by the Mah Jongg 1982
This edition first published 1987

British Library Cataloguing in Publication Data

Walters, Derek
Fortune-telling by Mah Jongg. — New ed.
1. Fortune-telling   2. Mah jongg
I. Title   II. Walters, Derek.
Your future revealed by the Mah Jongg
133.3'3   BF1891.M/

ISBN 0-85030-571-3

Printed and bound in Great Britain

FOR MY MOTHER AND FATHER

ACKNOWLEDGEMENTS

The author wishes to acknowledge the unflagging assistance given by staff at the Horniman Museum, Forest Hill, London; The Royal Asiatic Society, London; the Department of Oriental Antiquities, British Museum; the Department of Oriental Manuscripts and Printed Books, British Library; and the Royal Society of Arts, London.

My thanks are also due to Mrs Ursula Valentine, of Sark, who first taught me to play Mah Jongg, and to the following friends for their help and encouragement: Mr Peter Ashrif, Mr Ahmet Altuntash, Mr Dogan Ergun, Mr Trevor Huet, Miss Tsuneko Kubo, Mr David Mak, Mr Richard Moore, and Mrs Gwladys Newman.

The calligraphy in Part Two is by Mr David Yuk Kwan Mak.

CONTENTS

INTRODUCTION

(i) The Game of Mah Jongg

This book does not enter into the vexed question of the rules of Mah Jongg any more than a book on the Tarot would explain the rules of poker, or a guide to telling fortunes by dreams would give hints on the best way to get to sleep at night (as desirable though the latter may be). There are several books available concerning the rules of play for the game of Mah Jongg; the reader is most likely to encounter the following ones.

Of the obligatory instruction books included in new sets, the most curious is *Directions of playing Mah-Jongg, 'Chinese Game of Four Winds'*. My copy is anonymous and undated, and was given to me by a friend as a kind of linguistic curiosity. A. D. Millington (see below) identifies this as being published in Hong Kong. The text is identical to that in another pamphlet called *The Directions for Playing Mar Chuk*, which names the author or publisher as Kwong Hing Loong. It is still being distributed. Its advantage lies in the fact that the Chinese terms, with the Cantonese pronunciation, are given with the English terms alongside. Unfortunately, as my friend discovered to her chagrin, it does not actually explain how to play the game.

The book one is most likely to encounter in bookshops is a little volume which has been published more or less continuously since 1938, *The Game of Mah Jong* by W. Maxwell Robertson. This has been largely superseded by the extremely well-researched *The Complete Book of Mah-Jongg* by A. D. Millington, which sets out to be just what its title claims. This can be regarded as the standard work on the playing of Mah Jongg.

It is thoroughly indexed with English and Chinese glossaries, and dialect variants.

For those who do not wish to go to the expense of buying the Millington work, an equally up-to-date booklet is *Know the Game — Mah Jong* by Gwyn Hedley and Yvonne Seeley.

Mah Jongg: The Name

Throughout this book, the spelling 'Mah Jongg' has been used, simply because no such word as Jongg exists or is possible in Chinese. The choice is not through perversity; there are so many variants of the name in Chinese that the transcription Mah Jongg has been deliberately adopted to avoid lending weight to any of the several spellings in current use. 'Mah Jongg' was one of the titles given to the game when it was introduced to the West, as there was a danger that other transcriptions could contravene patents already taken out on the game by ambitious entrepreneurs who claimed to have invented it.

Having decided on the spelling of Mah Jongg, it is as well to be specific about its pronunciation, which is with a hard J, as in Jack. The word was originally transliterated by and for English speakers, for whom the letter J had a well-defined sound; so those who like to demonstrate their familiarity with foreign languages, whether German, French, Spanish or Japanese, by pronouncing 'Jongg' as Yong, Zhong, Hong, or even Rrong, should know that none of these comes anywhere near the original Chinese, which is more like the way Italians say 'Ciao!'. However, even allowing for dialect difference, there still remains considerable variation, not only in the pronunciation, but also the writing and even the meaning of Mah Jongg in Chinese.

Two possible characters can be ascribed to the first syllable, Mah. These are Ma (馬) horse, and Ma (麻) hemp. The former appears in what is perhaps the most likely source of the name, the card game Ma Tiao (麻弔). Ma, meaning horse, is not only the name of a chess piece, it is also the name of one of the combinations of dominoes used in divination (see below, page 40). Tiao, meaning to suspend, also means a string of cash (a string of Chinese copper coins which have square holes in the middle). 'Ma Tiao' could be a reference to the exchange of money at the end of the game. 'Tiao' itself might be a corruption of another syllable, such as Chiang (韁) meaning a bridle. This syllable, closely resembling the modern pronunciation which gave rise to 'Jongg', is the least fanciful of the possibilities. Ma Chiang, a horse's bridle, makes sense, even if the allusion is obscure. Other possibilities are Ch'iang (鎗)

meaning money, or Chiao (㑘) meaning luck, both of which might have allusions to the gambling aspects of the game. The latter pronunciation, closer to the 'Tiao' of the card game, can also be expressed by the character (交), meaning to pay, or to exchange, and might refer to the exchange of tiles throughout the course of the game.

Today however, virtually all Chinese sources give Ma (麻) hemp as the first syllable. This unfortunately does not indicate unanimity, because opinion on which character best represents the second syllable is divided between two schools of thought. One has it that the second syllable is (雀) Ch'iao (Ch'üeh, Ts'io or Ch'ioh), meaning small birds, while the second opts for (將) Chiang (Tsiang), to take. Ma Ch'iao (麻雀) literally hemp birds, actually means sparrows, and this meaning is the one most commonly offered as a translation of Mah Jongg. Oddly enough, it appears that the spelling most favoured by the Chinese is (麻將) Ma Chiang, hemp taking (which has no connection with drug-taking, note). However, if the latter character has the radical for gold added to it, this indicates a slight pronunciation change to Ch'iang(鏘) and the character can be read as tinkling or rustling. Ma Ch'iang (麻鏘) now takes on the meaning 'rustling of hemp leaves'.

Despite the present practice among the Chinese being to favour Ma = hemp as the first syllable, I tend to the view that the many links which Ma (馬) horse has with chess and dominoes are a strong indication that the original name of the game had some association with horses.

Elaborately ornamented horse's bridle of the Western Chou dynasty (841-770 B.C.). 'Mah Jongg' may be a corruption of the Chinese for 'horse's bridle'.

PART ONE:
A Brief History of Chinese Divination and Fortune-telling Games

1.

MAH JONGG:
HISTORY AND ANTECEDENTS

(i) Sticks and Stones (笑)

The game of Mah Jongg arrived in the West during the opening decades of the twentieth century; the rules of the game, and even the physical components of the game itself, did not become standardized until some forty or fifty years later, so it is all the more remarkable that the neatly-presented black padded box housing the mass-produced plastic pieces of the modern Mah Jongg set actually encapsulates not just a compendium of gambling games, but the implements for systems of Chinese divination that go back more than two thousand years. It is as if the whole of Chinese mystical thought and philosophy collected over the millenia had been timely distilled into that compact box at the very moment that a curtain was drawn over the last of the Chinese dynasties. The Mah Jongg tiles, the four dice, the counting sticks, and even the circular place markers are all tangible reminders of similar ancient devices depicted or described as early as the Han dynasty, two hundred years before the Christian era, while the nomenclature and other intangible aspects of Mah Jongg stem from traditions which are twice as old.

Mah Jongg belongs to that genus of games which includes cards, dominoes and even dice, but its pedigree is much more ancient. Though the history of its development occasionally leads into blind alleyways, it is a truly remarkable one, touching, as it does, upon astrology, chess, gambling, and, oddest of all, the Earth's magnetic field.

The greater part of present-day knowledge regarding the history of games stems from a significant exhibition staged in Atlanta and Chicago in 1893. Subsequently, this comprehensive collection of games from all over the world was moved to the United States National Museum, and was considerably expanded with the addition of many more items, making it one of the most exhaustive collections ever assembled. The compiler of the great catalogue, and the man in charge of the exhibition, was Dr Stewart Culin, then Director of the Museum of Archaeology and Palaeontology at the University of Pennsylvania. According to Dr Culin, the original aim in assembling the collection was to try and trace the possible origins of chess and playing cards. The results were to prove startling. One of the lines of investigation, suggested by Frank H. Cushing, was the possibility that chess and playing cards were both descended from arrow divination methods, which are not only found all over the globe, but are also of great antiquity, being mentioned in the Bible for example. This intriguing notion proved to be on the right lines, and in fact uncovered a complex network of associated ideas, leading to a theory that, with only slight modifications, is still accepted by scholars today. In brief, the eventual conclusions drawn from the study of that vast collection showed that all games such as chess, dice, dominoes and playing cards did indeed have their origins in divinatory practices that are still in use world-wide.

It is not a simple matter to demonstrate the family tree of gambling games and divination methods that led to the Mah Jongg as we know it today. There is no direct line of descent, but instead a myriad of cross-links that go back through centuries. Nor is it possible to point to a time and place from which all games and divination methods sprang. (The words 'chicken' and 'egg' come readily to mind.) It is perhaps simplest to outline some of the basic principles of those games and divination practices which are found throughout the world, and which are known to have existed at a very early date.

One of the most fundamental is that of throwing a number of sticks or twigs on the ground; these are then divided into groups of two at random, whereupon subsequent division of the sticks leads either to a remainder or not. This division-by-sticks process is universal, even though the rules regarding its operation, and indeed its object, vary considerably. In the well-known I Ching the number of sticks that remains after each operation determines the selection of lines in the hexagram. In other instances, the dividing of a number of sticks may be a game of counting skill, such as one can play with matches. In course of time, the sticks came to be used simply as counters to reckon the score in some other game — such as Mah Jongg. However, the original purpose of the sticks was not to act as a tally, but *to determine a number at random,* even though the result may simply be 1 or 0. A few more remarks on this subject are given later, in the paragraph on Yin and Yang, Part 2 (pp. 43-5).

This process is somewhat cumbersome, even time-consuming, though its use in the I Ching is a deliberate ploy to concentrate the mind of the person consulting the oracle. Subsequently, quicker methods of using the sticks were devised, such as that of notching or in other ways marking them, a practice still found among tribes in the North and South Americas, Africa, and Central Asia. In South China, one method of divination, Kua Tsim, uses bamboo splints tipped with red paint and bearing one of four markings: a dot, a double dot, a circle or a small cross. Even though there are only four types of marking, the number of splints used is either 32 or 64, an equal number of splints bearing each mark. The interpretation of these marks is as follows:

.	single — Yang	(大陽)
:	broken — Yin	(大陰)
o	doubled — lesser Yang	(小陽)
×	united — lesser Yin	(小陰)

Those who are familiar with the I Ching will see at once the connection between these marks and the formation of the trigrams and hexagrams of the I Ching, complete with the 'moving lines'. Another method of stick selection, which is more or less confined to China and neighbouring countries, is that called the Ch'ien (Chih, or Ts'ien)(籤). In this method the sticks are numbered from 1 to 100, one stick is shaken out of the bundle, and the oracle consulted by referring to a book with numbered pages. This method may seem simpler, but in fact presupposes a highly sophisticated method of reckoning, and a numerical notation which is considerably in advance of its primitive origins.

In contrast with the 'bundle of sticks' method of making a random choice is the one which uses only two objects. At its simplest it is two clenched fists, one of which holds a stone or some other small object. One development of this is the 'blind choice' between two similar but distinguishable objects — a short or a long straw, or two seeds of different colour. The classic example is the mysterious Urim and Thummim of the Bible, first mentioned in Exodus 28:30, and subsequently in six other places. The problem to scholars has always been that Urim and Thummim are plural words (like Cherubim and Seraphim), thus indicating not just a pair of objects, but several pairs. It may be, however, that the explanation is as simple as asking 'heads or tails?' when a (single) coin is thrown into the air.

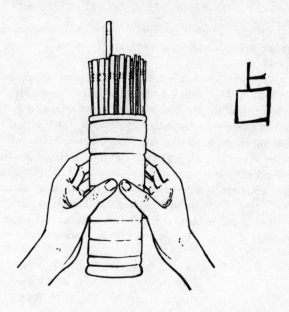

Figure 2. A box of divining stalks being shaken and the Chinese character for 'divination' (see frontispiece).

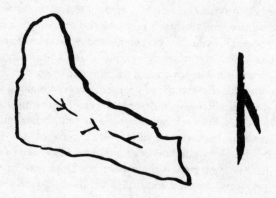

Figure 3. A shoulder bone, with cracks, used for divination, and the Chinese character for 'oracle' (see frontispiece).

Possibly similar to the Biblical Urim and Thummim is a method of divination used by the Chinese which is sometimes referred to as 'the divining dominoes'. These are known as Chiao or Kau (珓) and are two pieces of hard wood, or sometimes, as the Chinese character would seem to indicate, made of jade, shaped rather like a Brazil nut, flat on one side and convex on the other. (The characteristic curved back is of course one of the features which distinguished the Mah Jongg tile from Western dominoes.) Dr Culin described the use of the Chiao in a privately printed pamphlet *Religious and Magical Ceremonies in China* in the following way: 'It was growing dark when I entered the laundry, and the owner had let down his queue, put on his best robe, and was waiting with covered head to receive the cooked meats from the kitchen for sacrifice.' The owner, who had of course been expecting Dr Culin, then lighted two large painted candles and waved a bundle of incense three times before a shrine before displaying the smouldering incense sticks in front of representations of the different divinities. The Chiao P'ai (Kau Pui) (珓杯) were placed together, lifted above his head, and allowed to fall to the floor. The indications were one of three possibilities:

Both with curved sides uppermost	Yin Po (neither good nor bad)
Both with flat sides uppermost	Yang Po (unfavourable)
One flat, one round side uppermost	Chung Po (favourable)

The Chiao are thrown until three Yin, Yang, or Chung appear in succession. Whether Dr Culin recorded the use of the Chiao correctly is not known, but it would seem from the foregoing that the chances of a favourable reading are higher than the others, and an unfavourable reading only one in four; a very felicitous oracle indeed.

One might suppose that the reason for a weighting on the side of a favourable reading was due in no small measure to the purpose of the oracle, which was to determine whether or not one should proceed to the next stage of the divination. The use of coins to determine the lines of the I Ching hexagrams is a method related to the Chiao, except that three pieces are employed instead of two. The idea of calling 'heads or tails' is older than that of coin currency, since elaborately decorated flat discs, carved from wood or bone or even made in pottery, were produced exclusively for the purposes of casting lots in primitive societies that had not yet developed coinage as it is now known. Two developments now took place. The first of these was the extension of the function of the divination pieces along several different directions. The Chiao kind of piece, which could only determine one of two things (negative and positive, masculine and feminine, yin and yang) was superseded in some areas by knuckle bones, used as a kind of dice with four determinatives. It is easy to see how the approximately cubic shape of the knuckle bone should give rise to the present form of the dice, with its six regular faces producing six, equally-weighted determinatives. But before elaborating any further on the development of the dice into the domino and the playing card, a different line of development comes into consideration — the appearance of board games. Although it might appear that a playing board has very little to do with Mah Jongg, which does not use a board, it will shortly be seen that the terminology and method of play in the game of Mah Jongg owes a great deal to a primitive kind of board game, which had astrological as well as magical associations. An even more curious development, however, was the practical use which was eventually found for this board.

Figure 4. Pottery tomb figures of the Han dynasty playing Liu Po.
Photograph: British Museum.

(ii) The Game of Liu Po (六博)

There is no shortage of evidence to show that board games have been known for thousands of years. Many Egyptian examples exist, and there is even a famous beautifully-made example of a board game from Chaldean Ur which can be seen in the British Museum. All these games appear to have a similar principle to that of the well-known game of Ludo, itself a game of ancient origin but with surviving forms found in many different parts of the world today. A typical variant is the Korean game of Nyout, which uses pieces on a board moved along a circuit in accordance with the throw of a dice. The rules of the game, including the sending back of opponent's pieces if caught on the circuit, or the carrying forward of one's own doubled pieces, are almost exactly the same as those of Ludo.

In most board games, the focal point of interest lies on the board itself, so it is interesting to note the curious shift in emphasis in such games as dominoes, or cards, which use a cribbage board. Here the board has been reduced in status to that of a mere tally, and the entertainment in these games lies in the skill with which the players are able to manipulate the numbers they have been dealt.

A totally different kind of board was in use in ancient Chinese times for astronomical, calendrical and possibly even horary reckoning long before it had been demoted to the status of a gaming board. This was the Shih (式), and although there are numerous accounts regarding the appearance and function of the Shih, no actual example has been found. Attempts to reconstruct a model of the Shih have taken into account all the classical references to it, as well as the elaborate form of extant geomantic boards which it is believed are the descendants of the Shih. According to several writers, playing pieces Ch'i (棋, 棊, or 碁) were thrown on to the board, and in some way the pieces were moved around to represent conjunctions of the stars and planets. What is certain is that the board was aligned with the points of the compass, and may even have been used as a sundial. Several other factors, including the representation of the stars of Ursa Major (the Great Bear) in the centre of the board, will be discussed more fully later on. The interesting thing is that the oldest representations of a Chinese playing board do not have these marks on them, but instead show other, so far unexplained, signs quite clearly and consistently. This game, for which there is ample reference in Chinese literature, is the game of Liu Po (六博), usually translated as the game of the Six Learned Scholars (but which I prefer to translate as the game of the Six Wisdoms). In the British Museum there is a charming group of pottery figures from a Han Dynasty (202 B.C.-

A.D.220) tomb who are shown playing Liu Po, or rather, two are playing the game while a third watches over. Both players have six pieces lined up in front of them; at the back of the board are six sticks, called Chu (箸) (the word, meaning 'bamboo things', is identical with the word for chopsticks). Throwing these Chu determines the moves of the Ch'i. Commentaries on the game also refer to a central river, on reaching which the Ch'i were promoted, and, further, that the Ch'i were marked with representations of the four mythical beasts ruling the points of the compass — the Blue Dragon (East), the Vermilion Bird (South), the White Tiger (West) and the Black Warrior, sometimes known as Tortoise (North). The use of these names is significant.

There are several representations of the Liu Po board in existence. The clearest is the one shown in the pottery tomb figures in the British Museum. In this group the board, set out on a low table, clearly has two functions. It is twice as long as it is broad, and can be thought of as being two large squares, although there is no actual dividing line between the two halves of the board. On one of these half-boards the six Chu are laid out in lines. These Chu, and the half-board on which they are laid, do not appear in other representations of the Liu Po game which have been found. Among the pottery figures which constitute the little group is a small vase known as Hu (壺), the significance of which seems to have been overlooked by researchers. One of the Chinese Classics, the Li Chi, or Book of Rites, dating from the late Han dynasty, which is from about the same period as the group of pottery figures, describes at great length a form of divination in which arrows are cast into a pot, Chou Shih (籌矢), literally, to calculate by arrows. Several more references to this practice, whether as a game of skill, like darts, or as a form of divination, can be found in other Chinese essays spanning a dozen or more centuries from 529 B.C. onwards. The fact that this harks back to Culin and Cushing's thesis that all games are ultimately derived from arrow divination will not have escaped notice; but what is more significant is that the Chinese character for the action of throwing the arrows into the pot, T'ou (投), should be the same as that for casting the Ch'i on to the divining board. We have therefore encountered a game which stands at the crossroads of two distinct divination procedures: one by arrows, and the other by movable pieces.

Turning to look at the other half of the board — the side used for the game of Liu Po itself, the first thing to notice is that it is not a chequered board such as might be used for chess, draughts, or the well-known Japanese game of Go, which had its origins in the Chinese game of Wei Ch'i (圍棋). Nor does it have any circuit or route along which the

Figure 5. Typical design on the back of a Han Dynasty mirror.

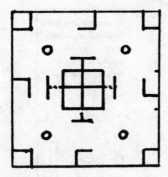

Figure 6. Representation of a divining board from a Wu Liang tomb, Han Dynasty, *circa* A.D. 147.

pieces might be moved, as can be seen in the Chaldean playing board. What the board does have, and quite unmistakably, is a series of marks at each corner, and at each edge. These are referred to by sinologists as TLV marks on account of their resemblance to those letters. Their rectangular form is quite unlike anything else found in Chinese art, whether as part of the script or the design. They are almost a standard feature of the decoration of ancient bronze mirror backs, but have also been found elsewhere (in tomb carvings, for example). Their frequent association with ancient sundials has led to the belief that they might have some significance with regard to the alignment of the sundial with the points of the compass. The question which frequently arises is therefore, what was the origin of these angular marks which are found on the backs of mirrors, on sundials, and on the board of a game which had mystical significance?

Figure 7. A Ching Dynasty coin. Note the overall similarity in shape to the Han mirror. The inscription reads: '[Emperor] K'ien Lung: True Currency', which dates the coin A.D. 1736-96.

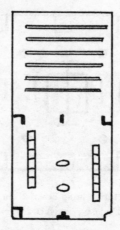

Figure 8. Diagram of the markings on the Liu Po board, made in glazed pottery, associated with two pottery figures from a Han Dynasty tomb. The original can be seen in the British Museum.

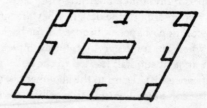

Figure 9. Isometric view of a divining board, perhaps indicating that it was meant to be tilted. From a detail in the decoration of a Han Dynasty mirror.

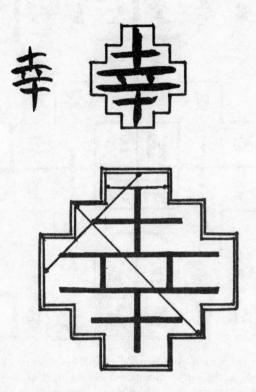

Figure 10. The character Hsing, meaning 'Good Fortune', and a construction
showing how it may be related to the divining board.

Quite by chance, a solution presented itself to me from an entirely
unexpected quarter. While preparing some diagrams to accompany an
article on Chinese astrology, I wondered whether it would be possible to
construct a chart that would satisfactorily align the twenty-eight houses
of the Chinese map of the heavens with the twelve Chinese hour signs
and the four points of the compass. There is, alas, not enough scope
within the present work to enlarge on the details of why I felt this to be
necessary, nor how I arrived at a solution. Suffice it to say that it was
reached when I eventually divided a large square into 64 smaller squares
— the resemblance to a chess board was not to occur to me until later —
and allocated one of the twenty-eight constellations to each of the

Figure 11. The author's reconstruction of the Han Dynasty divining board. The TLV marks fence off the four quadrants and indicate the four cardinal lunar mansions. The horary signs run clockwise and begin in the top right-hand segment (midnight). The twenty-eight Hsui run anti-clockwise and begin to the right of the base centre mark.

squares along the edges of the larger square. The points of the compass and the twelve hour signs fitted compactly into this new format; it only remained necessary, for greater clarity, to thicken the boundaries of some of the small squares so as to emphasize the relationships which existed between the various figures in the chart. It was while I was doing this that the similarity of the chart to the Liu Po board suddenly became apparent. I then compared the new chart with a copy of the Liu Po board as represented in some Han dynasty tomb carvings, and noticed that where four blank squares appeared in the new chart, four small circles were shown on the Han board. Quite possibly these holes could have been for sighting pins if the board was to be used for calculating true North, or true noon, in the manner of a sextant or sundial.

A curious coincidence, bearing out the connection of the board both with astronomical observation, divination and gaming, was that the pattern formed by the boundary of the horary signs as they were arranged on the new chart produced a stylized form of the Chinese character Hsing (幸) meaning Good Fortune. It would be extremely appropriate if the sign for Good Fortune — a popular motif in Chinese decoration, should have its origins in the formal pattern that arose at the centre of that most ancient of astrological computers, held equally in awe by gambler and seer.

(iii) Lo P'an (羅盤)

The Shih continued to evolve, taking two different lines of development. One was into board games of the chess genre, and the other into the Lo P'an, or Geomancer's Compass.* This latter was the instrument used in the Chinese magical art of Feng Shui (風水), a branch of the divinatory arts which is totally without equivalent in the West. It was used principally for pointing out the best site for a tomb, house, or some other kind of construction. Belief in Feng Shui was very strong, right up to the present century, and proved a great obstacle to the pioneers of railway construction in China, since very often the most expedient route for a railway line did not match the lines of force which were believed to be in accordance with the principles of Feng Shui. Here is another instance of the board being used in connection with the orientation of the four cardinal points, and because they have retained such a dominant role in the game of Mah Jongg it is worth investigating this a little further.

At some stage in the development of the Shih, it became the custom to spin a spoon round on its bowl, and observe the direction in which the handle pointed. No doubt generations of parents have before and since been irritated by their children discovering this little trick for themselves. The reasons for spinning the spoon on the Shih, however, were much more profound. The ancient Chinese astronomers used a quite different method of observation to that of the astronomers of Babylonian times. Of paramount importance in the Chinese celestial sphere was the Pole Star, and the constellation Ursa Major which pointed to it. To the Chinese this constellation, known in the West as the Great Bear, was known, and still is, as the Ladle. The configuration of the seven stars which make up the Ladle therefore had considerable significance; it was at least one of the most recognizable constellations in the night sky, and for this reason it was often found depicted on religious

*See photograph p. 72.

flags. It was natural, therefore, for this group of stars to be depicted at the centre of the Shih. The next step was the inclusion of an actual ladle as a spinning pointer — a tangible representation of a heavenly, and therefore mystical, phenomenon. It seems significant that the Chinese character for North (北) (Pei) should consist of two characters for Spoon, Pi (匕), placed back to back, although the usual historical reason given for the character is that it represents two men standing back to back.

Then there came a dramatic innovation. The spinning spoon was replaced by a very special kind of spoon, one that must at first have surely been regarded as having magical properties, for it was made from lodestone, and after it had been set spinning would always come to rest pointing in the same direction. (I cannot help feeling that, human nature being what it is, some unscrupulous diviners or gaming masters may have used the secret of the lodestone to effect their own ends!)

(iv) Chessmen and Playing Pieces (象棊)

The lodestone introduces the subject of magnetism into what is already a somewhat involved and tortuous history, but the relevance will be seen in a moment. There are five extant versions in classical literature of a curious incident which happened at least two centuries before the Christian era. In brief, the story is that the Han emperor Wu asked his court magician to demonstrate his automatic 'chessmen' (Ch'i — a word which will be explained later). It has been supposed that these were lodestone 'men' on a board which could be set to move by moving other pieces of magnet beneath the board — a familiar enough children's toy today, but an extraordinary wonder in those far-off times. That the 'chessmen' must have been some kind of playing piece, and not some ingenious mechanical toy is shown by the character Ch'i, which is the character used for playing pieces of a board game, as distinct from pieces (such as cards or Mah Jongg tiles) used in games without a board. The character Ch'i has three variants, all of which mean exactly the same, (棋) or (棊), and (碁). In the first two versions, the radical 'wood' is shown either to the left or underneath another part of the character which is a pronoun. The third variant of the character Ch'i (碁) uses the radical for 'stone' in place of the 'wood' radical, which seems to indicate that in early versions of the game either stone or wooden pieces were used.

The word Ch'i has now become almost synonymous with chess. At a very early stage the word Hsiang (象) came to be used to mean games such as chess which were played with a *variety* of pieces as distinct from games such as draughts or ludo which are played with *similar* pieces. Hsiang originally meant elephant, doubtless named after one of the pieces in the game, and eventually, because the Hsiang (elephant chess piece) was a model of a larger object in the real world, the word Hsiang came to mean a model or a symbol. Later the word Hsiang in its figurative sense was distinguished from the literal meaning by having the radical for 'man' added to it (像). However, in the I Ching the character is still written in the old style, which accounts for the curious introduction to each of the commentaries: 'The Elephant says . . .'.

In the earliest forms of Hsiang, the pieces represented heavenly objects — the Sun, Moon, and constellations — and were thrown on to some form of playing board. There is no shortage of references to Hsiang in the later classical works; obviously the game was considered to be of great antiquity even then. Sadly, no contemporary literature on the game has survived, although fortunately the preface still exists to a Hsiang manual which is no longer extant. This was a manual written by the Emperor Wu of the Northern Chou dynasty (reigned A.D. 561-578), and it is recorded that the game was considered of such importance that he used to lecture to his courtiers on the philosophy inherent in the game. The preface to the Emperor's manual The Chess Classic, Hsiang Ching (象經) was written by an authority on divination games, Wang Pao, who lived at about the same time as the Emperor. From Wang Pao we learn that the game was regarded as a kind of allegory of Heaven and Earth. Similarly, it taught the principles of Yin and Yang, the Seasons and the Colours, the Five Elements, the Musical Tones, the Eight Diagrams of the I Ching, Loyalty and Filial Piety, Rulers and Ministers, Peace and War, Rites and Ceremonies, Recognition of Virtue and Punishment of Vice. One or two of these topics will be covered at greater length in the next section. For the moment, there are some observations arising out of Wang Pao's comments which can be made on this early game.

Some of Wang Pao's categories, such as the teaching of Loyalty and Filial Piety, seem to foreshadow those ambitious Victorian attempts to instil moral virtues by means of 'improving' board games: the Samaritans advance two squares, the Wicked miss a turn. Other categories need further explanation. Heaven was represented by those pieces which bore the names of celestial bodies — the Sun, Moon, and so forth — and also by the configuration of pieces on the board, since these were apparently taken to represent certain constellations. Other Ch'i, symbolizing the Five Elements (fire, earth, water, wood, and metal) represented the Earth. Heaven and Earth were also symbolized by the Yin and Yang of the odd and even numbers respectively. (This needs further comment, since in most parallels between numbers and the Yin and Yang, it is the odd numbers which represent Heaven, Yang, and the even numbers Earth and Yin.) More importantly, however, is that the mention of numbers makes an immediate distinction between Hsiang games and modern chess; modern chess has no numerical function, and so there would have been little point in drawing parallels between odd numbers and Heaven, or even numbers and the Earth. Conversely, numbers and computation feature very strongly in the game of Mah Jongg. But perhaps the most arresting category is the one of which Wang Pao says: 'The fourth [educational aspect of Hsiang] teaches the Seasons, the colour of the East being Green, with the other directions also having their proper colours.' Here is a direct link between the points of the compass, colours, and the seasons of the year, just as there is in the game of Mah Jongg. Another of Wang Pao's categories also brings Mah Jongg to mind. This is his eleventh, 'concerning Rites and Ceremonies', for it is certainly a fact that Mah Jongg is invested with a kind of ritual, or ceremonial form of playing. Indeed, this is one of the game's chief attractions as a pastime. Only when the game descends into an obsessive gambling medium is this gentler, more formal side, of Mah Jongg lost.

Wang Pao also wrote commentaries on another game using a board similar to the Shih. This was T'an Ch'i (彈棊), a term almost untranslatable in that the first character signifies a bolt fired from a crossbow, and the second a playing piece; 'Bullet-chess' is the literal but meaningless translation. It seems to be as old as Liu Po, and shares similarities with that game in that it had twelve pieces, six for each player. The T'an Ch'i pieces, coloured red and black, sometimes bore symbols relating to the twelve calendrical animals (rat, ox, and so on).

Books from the same period also refer to Ling Ch'i (靈棊) (Spirit Ch'i), another divination game using twelve pieces. These were marked Shang (上) (ascending), Chung (中) (centre), and Hsia (下) (descending). There were four of each, and a parallel with the Fa (發), Chung (中), and Pai (白) (blank) tiles of Mah Jongg is immediately apparent. The Ling Ch'i, known to Tung Fang Shuo, adviser to Emperor Wu of the Han dynasty 141-87 B.C., was evidently of great antiquity even in the eighth century A.D., when the earliest extant essay on the subject, the Ling Ch'i Ching (靈棊經), came to be included in the collection of Taoist classics. These early essays, describing the auguries of various combinations of Shang, Chung, and Hsia, are the prototypes of the Spirit Books, Ling Chieng (靈籤), which are used by

Chinese fortune-tellers today. The Ling Ch'i were thrown on to a board — one commentary notes that it was *round*, to represent Heaven — and the combinations noted. The Ch'i in this case may have been flat discs, or temple tokens. Equally, they could have been shown by some kind of dice or tee-to-tum, since all that was needed was a combination of four sets of Shang, Chung, and Hsia. One hundred and twenty-five permutations are possible. The easiest way to obtain one of these combinations is to throw four cubic dice, each marked with three pairs of symbols. But dice were comparatively late in reaching China and may not have arrived until the invention of block printing. Had dice reached China during the Han dynasty they could have altered the manner in which the I Ching was consulted, the complex procedures with yarrow stalks or willow wands giving way to the much more convenient method of throwing four dice. This, however, is only conjecture. Yarrow stalks did not give way to dice, and one likely reason is that dice were not known in China until the yarrow stalk methods had become firmly established. How dice got to China, and the route by which they arrived, is not clear. They may have reached China via Tibet, where they were known until the middle of the last century almost exclusively for the purposes of divination.

(v) Dice, Playing Cards and Dominoes (牌)

Dice, therefore, arrived in China at a time in its history when a new invention was making its impact — that of printing. The two notions fused, giving rise to two related, but dissimilar, offspring: dominoes and cards. The six spots of the dice are after all very similar to the six spots on the domino, and one domino can convey the same information as two dice. A domino, furthermore, continues to display this information when laid on the table, picked up and put down again. Two dice, once re-shaken, may or may not still show the original combination of spots. It is the manipulation of the pieces — the rules of the game — which determines whether dice or dominoes are adopted. By the same token, playing cards also show two pieces of information — the suit and the number of the card, although these two pieces of information do not belong to the same category, in the sense that on a five-six domino, say, the five and six belong to the same 'set' of numbers. In standard playing cards there are two 'sets', numbers and suits, while in the Tarot there are three: the numbers, suits, and the Major Arcana.

To summarize these points: dice, dominoes and playing cards can be defined as three categories of game that do not use a playing board and that can be distinguished not by their shape, but by the information which the pieces convey. Dice display single pieces of information, which are lost once the dice are rolled; dominoes display and retain two pieces of information of the same class; cards display two pieces of information of different classes.

Although they have their standard forms, all three categories have their variants, such as poker or crown and anchor dice, six-or nine-spot dominoes, and standard, Tarot, or even Lexicon cards. From this classification it follows that Mah Jongg falls into the playing card category, with three suits in place of the four in standard or Tarot cards, honours tiles (Fa, Chung, Pai, North, East, South and West) in place of the court cards, and the Seasons and Flowers in place of the Major Arcana of the Tarot. In other words, it is the shape of the Mah Jongg tile alone which is its distinguishing feature. No Western games have pieces of this shape, whereas, to judge from the Han dynasty pottery figures, Chinese gentlemen of two thousand years ago were familiar with games using pieces of almost the same size and shape.

The Chinese word P'ai (牌) applies equally to cards, dominoes, or Mah Jongg tiles, dominoes being sometimes called (牙牌) Ya P'ai (ivory cards) or (骨牌) Ku P'ai (bone cards) in order to distinguish them from plain cards, revealing at once the common origin of all these games. According to several traditions, P'ai were invented during the reign of Chao Tsung, A.D. 1127-1163. Strangely enough, since the antiquity of traditions is usually greatly exaggerated, it can be shown that this date is in fact far too conservative an estimate of the actual antiquity of P'ai — dominoes or cards. W. H. Wilkinson, who was British Consul at Seoul in the late nineteenth century, and himself quite an authority on Chinese games (he contributed several items to Dr Culin's collection), suggests that the frequent references to a date of 1120 or thereabouts, given in several early Chinese encyclopaedias, refers not so much to the invention of P'ai as to a ratification of the rules of the game, in particular to the game T'ien Ch'iu (Heavens and Nines). There is a parallel with Mah Jongg, a game whose rules have only in the last dozen years or so crystallized into an internationally accepted standard.

Certainly P'ai were in use as early as the tenth century A.D. They are specifically referred to in the Liao Shih, (遼史), a historical record begun in A.D. 916. But more remarkable are the two tablets of Fu Hsi, of mythical origin but certainly very ancient indeed. Their appearance (according to the diagrams depicted in the I Ching) resembles nothing so much as the arrangements of spots on a dice or a domino. Of course, it can be argued that these arrangements were based on the Fu Hsi tablets, but the similarity is undeniable.

Dice

Chinese dice are similar to European dice in many respects, although closer observation will reveal that if a Chinese dice is held with the 1 uppermost, and the 2 facing, then 4 is to the left and 3 to the right, the reverse of European dice. On Chinese dice, the 1 is much larger than the other spots. Several imaginative explanations have been proposed to account for this oddity, but the truth is much more practical. Were the 1 not so heavily incised, the dice would be unbalanced by the lighter 6-spot side, which is the 1's opposite face. (As in European dice, the opposite faces add up to seven.)

Formerly, the 1 and 4 on a Chinese dice were marked in red, which divides the numbers 1 to 6 into two sets of three, each beginning with a red number, although recent practice is to engrave only the 1 in red. It is usually said that the 1 is engraved in red because the one black spot on a white background would be unlucky; the character Chu●, meaning a flame, being associated with the death of a parent. Two legends account for the engraving of the 4 in red, both of which are briefly related here for the sake of completeness. It is said that an emperor, dicing with his empress, won through an unexpectedly lucky succession of 4s, whereupon he ordered that the 4 should thenceforth be marked in red. Unfortunately, the emperors to whom this promulgation has been variously attributed belonged to wildly different epochs; either the Ming (明) (1638-1643) or the Chung Tsing (中宗) (684-710) — a mere discrepancy of some thousand years — which sheds some doubt on the veracity of this tale.

Another legend, charming even if not true, tells of a girl who was betrothed to a man whom she loved, but on her father's death was to be sold by her brother to the highest bidder. However, she ingeniously arranged that she would accept only the suitor who was successful in throwing three 4s in succession at dice. Naturally, when it was her betrothed's turn, she substituted loaded dice. The legend does not tell us whether she had also painted the 4 of the loaded dice in red, or why, out of the six numbers available, she should have chosen 4.

Chinese dicing games usually involve the throwing of more than one dice. Throwing pairs ties up with dominoes; alignments of 3s and 4s with Mah Jongg and similar games. Some of the combinations of numbers shown by dice have evocative names; for example, 1, 2, 3 is called Dancing Dragon, and 4, 5, 6 the Flower Necklace. The following pairs are of particular interest, since the first four names are also given to dominoes that have those pairs of numbers on their faces: 6-6, Heaven; 1-1, Earth; 4-4, Man; 1-3, Harmony; 5-5, Plum; 2-2, Bench; 5-6, Tiger's Head.

These names are significantly reminiscent of astrological terms, and are obviously a reference to the original use of dice for divination. It must be stressed that in some Eastern countries — especially Tibet — the use of dice was exclusively for fortune-telling, a diametrically opposite situation to that in the West, where they are scarcely, if ever, used for divination. A glance at the illustration of a Tibetan fortune-teller's dice will show why. It is difficult enough to imagine how this dice could be used for fortune-telling, let alone gambling. One prediction is sure: if used for gambling it would certainly give rise to considerable argument.

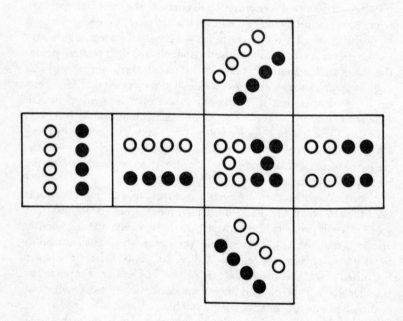

Figure 12. Tibetan Fortune-teller's Dice. *(Partly conjecture; it is not certain which of the faces are adjacent to which.)*

Dominoes

In some Mah Jongg sets, the Ch'ou (籌), counting sticks or tallies, (equivalent to what gamblers would call the 'chips') are based on old Chinese dominoes in design. They would not serve as dominoes, however, since they are usually engraved on both of the curved sides. The four tallies supplied with old Mah Jongg sets represent the double six, the double four, the double one, and the one/three. Like several other varieties of Chinese dominoes, each pair of numbers is marked at each end, instead of (as in the European domino) one of each pair at either end. That is to say, the Chinese one/three domino is marked one/three at each end; eight spots in all. These four tallies were popularly called by their equivalent domino names:

double six	T'ien	Heaven	(天)
double one	Ti	Earth	(地)
double four	Jen	Man	(人)
one/three	Ho	Harmony	(和)

These names were borrowed from the popular game of Heavens and Nines, already mentioned, which often appears in Chinese romantic literature (as, for example, the eighteenth-century novel by Tsao Hsueh-Chin, *A Dream of Red Mansions*).

The basic set of dominoes for Heavens and Nines consisted of sixteen pieces; four sixes, four ones, four fours, and four one/threes, this set being repeated either twice to make a set of thirty-two dominoes, or four sets making a total of sixty-four dominoes.

A second arrangement of dominoes consists of the following pyramid:

1:1	1:2	1:3	1:4	1:5	1:6
	2:2	2:3	2:4	2:5	2:6
		3:3	3:4	3:5	3:6
			4:4	4:5	4:6
				5:5	5:6
					6:6

This makes a total of twenty-one dominoes. The ones and fours are coloured red, as Chinese dice. It follows that this arrangement of dominoes is actually very similar to the European set, except that there are no blanks, and, as mentioned above, the dominoes are engraved at each end with both figures. This in fact has considerable strategic importance in their role as gaming pieces, for it is not possible to play the most popular European domino games with Chinese dominoes, *since it is not possible to match up the ends* for form a chain. The absence of the double blanks puts Chinese dominoes much closer to dice than European ones.

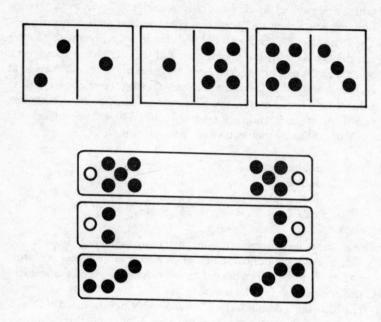

Figure 13. Diagram showing European and Chinese dominoes.

The dealer of the dominoes is sometimes called the 'Builder of the Barn' or 'Keeper of the Granary', Chu Ts'ang (築倉), and often has a small disc of wood in front of him to indicate that he is the dealer.

When the dominoes are used for what many authorities consider their original purpose, divination, the inquirer shuffles the dominoes with their faces down and arranges them into sets of three. The scores are totalled, and if this amounts to 32, this is regarded as a good omen; higher and lower scores indicate more or less likelihood of success or failure in the enterprise. This is in effect the overall result, but the process is much more complex. Because of the direct relevance to Mah Jongg divination methods, it is worth studying some of the details and the scoring methods.

Three dominoes, which together show one of each of the numbers 1 to 6, are called Pu T'ung (不同) (None Similar), and score the maximum

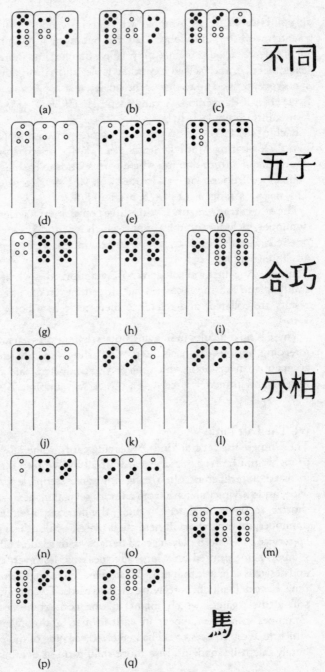

Figure 14. Examples of scoring in Chinese domino divination.

six points (see Figure 14, examples a, b, and c). Two identical doubles and a match with the third domino, so that out of the six numbers five are identical, are called Wu Tzu (五子) (Five Similar) and score five points (examples d, e, and f). Two identical doubles and a third domino whose spots together add up to one of the singles, (e.g. a 2/3 and two double-fives) are called Ingenious Arrangement, Ho Ch'iao (合巧) and score four points (example, g, h, i).

Each of the following arrangements scores three points: Fen Hsiang (分相), Sharing Mutually (examples j, k, l). This has two different doubles, and a third domino which corresponds to each double (e.g. a double-two, a double-one, and a one-two); Ma (馬), Horse (example m). This has an arrangement of 4/5, 5/6 and 6/4.

The other arrangements scoring three points are any selection of three dominoes, including doubles or not, which 1, 2, and 3, appearing twice; or else 2, 3, and 6, and any double (for examples, see n, o, p, and q); or any three matching pairs.

In the 'long method' of domino divination, the whole process of shuffling and scoring is carried out three times in all, after which the results are collated, and reference then made to a book of sybilline verses.

There is no difficulty in imaging how a divination system such as the foregoing, with its emphasis on 'scoring', should readily lend itself to a competitive diversion in which the players competed, paid and received forfeits, and ultimately used it as a vehicle for gambling.

(vi) The Last Links

The Chinese use several kinds of playing cards, some of which would probably not be recognized as cards at all by Western players. Their format is quite different, often being long narrow strips, less than an inch wide, and varying in length from a few to several inches — usually, the shorter, the later the date. On some, the markings are reminiscent of dominoes; on others, of Chinese chess pieces, while others seem to pay lip-service to Western playing card designs, with spade, club and other symbols being printed on. Generally speaking, however, their format and design is so exotic that most Westerners, on seeing them for the first time, have difficulty in perceiving them as cards. To complicate matters still further, games which might in one context be considered as dominoes sometimes appear in card format, and conversely, games which to Western eyes could be perceived as being of the playing card family might be made up in a more solid form as dominoes. This of course accounts for the considerable variety of styles and designs in both dominoes and Chinese cards.

The first games to be recognizably similar to Mah Jongg were shown at the 1893 exhibitions and can be referred to as the 'Wilkinson' and 'Glover' sets on account of the fact that they were respectively donated by W. H. Wilkinson, formerly British Consul at Seoul, and the other by George B. Glover, the United States Consul at Foochow.

The pieces in the Wilkinson set were approximately the same size as a Mah Jongg piece, but are clearly related to what would be dominoes by Western criteria. There were six ranks (some authorities say 'suits', but this is patently the wrong term) of twenty-one pieces, equivalent to the Chinese dominoes described in the previous section. The first three ranks were marked with spots, in red and black in the usual manner. Two ranks were additionally engraved with flowers in red and green, and the sixth rank had representations of the eight genii of Chinese mythology, the Sun, Moon, Tiger and several flowers engraved between the double sets of spots. Four pieces were marked Fa (發), commonly known as the 'green dragon' in Mah Jongg, but meaning 'commence'.

The Glover set was almost identical to the Mah Jongg set of today, with a few significant details differentiating it. It consisted of four suits of rectangles, 1-9 (the equivalent of Mah Jongg bamboos), four suits of circles 1-9, and four suits of myriads, 1-9 (the latter suits identical with Mah Jongg pieces). The rectangles were marked in red and green, the circles in red, green and blue, and the myriads in blue. There were also four of each of the four cardinal points, and four Chung (中) (known in common parlance as the 'red dragon'). What is very interesting, however, is that the Chung was engraved in blue, the same as the four cardinal points, so showing that the Chung was originally conceived as one of the *five* cardinal points known to the Chinese way of thinking — North, South, East, West and Centre. The set also had eight blanks; these may well have been spares, or else four of the blanks may have been used in the game; they have been adopted into modern play as 'white dragons'. Chinese players, however, still refer to these as blank, or white, Pai (白). The Glover set had a further nine pieces which do not exist in modern Mah Jongg sets, but which may have been transformed into the Seasons and Garden tiles. These were the Five Governors, one for each of the (five) cardinal points and a further four: the Heavenly Governor, Earthly Governor, Mankind Governor, and Harmony Governor. The connection with Chinese dice and domino games is immediately apparent.

The curious intermingling of dice, dominoes, cards and Mah Jongg has not ceased. Early in 1981 I decided to take a short holiday in Turkey, a country which I had not visited for several years. During my early visits to the country, one of the favourite pastimes provided by the little cafés in every village was the game of backgammon. Much to my surprise, on my 1981 visit, I saw that Turkish menfolk were now in the grip of a new craze: elli-bir (fifty-one), which outwardly showed every similarity to Mah Jongg. It used tiles — rather flatter than Mah Jongg pieces, being 32×27×5cm — and these were displayed on racks in front of each player. The tiles were numbered from 1-13 in four colours, with the addition of a sun symbol which acted as a joker in the game, and there were two 'packs' of identical tiles. In other words, the tiles represented nothing more than two ordinary packs of playing cards, with the numbers 11-13 replacing the Jack, Queen and King.

I was told that the game had been known in Turkey for 'several' years, but it could not have been more than five or six years old. Certainly the game was unknown in the 1960s. Another curious fact is that the game must have been of Turkish origin, since the tiles and racks had been manufactured in that country. Very shortly after my return from Turkey, I was astonished to find my godchildren playing the game in London; they had been sent a handsomely boxed set of 'tile rummy' from their grandparents in Germany. The game is now to be seen in high-class games shops everywhere. The astonishing ubiquity of the game in Turkey, as well as its sudden emergence from absolutely nowhere, corresponds very clearly to the sudden and perplexing emergence of Mah Jongg at the beginning of this century.

Fu Hsi (see pp. 34, 36).

2.

SOME ASPECTS OF CHINESE PHILOSOPHY

All forms of Chinese divination are inextricably interwoven in a way that might seem inconceivable to a serious Western practitioner. The latter, if he were an astrologer, would not require to inspect his client's palms and finger-nails, call upon the spirits and then read the Tarot before actually getting down to casting the horoscope. Yet for the Chinese, such courses of action would not just be commonplace; they would be expected. A Chinese astrologer would be as well versed in the arts of I Ching, Feng Shui, Divination by Characters, Plant Stalks, Dominoes and all the other branches of the Chinese occult, as in his own special study.

For this reason, the following background paragraphs have been included to give some insight into those aspects of philosophy and belief which are peculiar to the Chinese, in order for the reader to have greater empathy with their divination methods.

(i) Yin and Yang (陰陽)

According to Chinese tradition, all things were produced from the Ultimate Limit by separation into Yin and Yang (陰陽). Originally, there was a single, undivided 'one-ness', which existed outside Time or Space; nothing, in fact. The creation of anything at all, whether merely the passage of time, or the existence of the space in which time passed, could only occur if there was non-space and non-time with which to make the comparison — like the vexing question, what is not nothing? Any positive action of existence was termed Yang, and its converse was

Yin. As Yang moved forwards, so Yin was the retreating; if Yang were existence, then Yin was not-existence. The two were opposites, but not in opposition; they were mutually dependent. Yang could not exist without Yin; they represented action and reaction. If there was heat, there had to be cold for the heat to be hotter than; if there was light, there must be darkness for the light to shine in. If there were no light, there could be no darkness; until there was light, darkness did not exist.

All Chinese natural philosophy conceived of the universe in terms of Yang combined with Yin. The Sun in its progress through the heavens moved from Yin into Yang, from winter into summer, thence to winter, back into Yin. Dynasties rose and fell in accordance with the same principle. No sooner is there completion than there is rebirth. These 'changes' came about through a four-stage cosmological process: (1) Li (理) order; (2) Shu (數) number; (3) Ch'i (氣) breath, motion, or spirit; (4) Hsing (形) form. Although this concept is literally thousands of years old, it is remarkable not only for its astuteness and absolute lack of superstitious belief, but for its extraordinarily scientific accuracy. These terms were translated long before anything was known about nuclear theory; a twentieth-century interpretation of these four concepts could just as well be: (1) Li, the physical laws of science; (2) Shu, mathematical constants and equations; (3) Ch'i, energy; and (4) Hsing, matter. The four ancient terms are an expression of Einstein's $e = mc^2$: or, in literary terms, the relationship between matter and energy is governed by physical laws. Furthermore, it is only within the past few decades that nuclear physicists have shown that all matter and all energy have positive and negative qualities. Scientists are today on the verge of isolating anti-matter, the existence of which was predicted by nuclear theorists whose hypotheses were formerly regarded as extravagant. Yet three thousand years ago, the existence of anti-matter was entirely logical to the Chinese, for it fitted in perfectly with their concepts of Yin and Yang.

Since everything consisted of Yin and Yang, it followed that Yin and Yang must themselves be capable of division into Yin and Yang, and that these divisions could be divided still further into sub-divisions, and so on ad infinitum. In point of fact, this same theory was rediscovered some two thousand years later by the seventeenth-century philosopher Gottfried Wilhelm von Leibniz while he was developing his system of binary numbers in 1679. (This system of counting uses only two numbers, 1 and 0, the numbers 1 to 8, for example, being expressed as follows: 1, 10, 11, 100, 101, 110, 111, 1000. This is the system which is used by computers, since 1 and 0 can be expressed simply as 'on' and 'off'). Leibniz considered his invention to have tremendous philosophical implications, since ultimately everything might be expressed as Being or Not Being, Yes and No. To Leibniz's astonishment, shortly after he had published his theory he received a letter from a Jesuit missionary in China, one Father Joachim Bouvet, who pointed out that the Chinese had been familiar with such a system of philosophy for nigh on three thousand years!

(ii) The Eight Diagrams (八卦)

Yin and Yang were expressed diagrammatically by Yao (爻), or lines, broken ones for Yin (--) and unbroken ones for Yang (—). Groups of lines, usually three or six, were called Kua (卦), commonly translated as 'diagrams' or, more specifically, trigrams if three lines are used, hexagrams if there are six, as in the I Ching. Three Yao can be combined in eight different ways — the Eight Diagrams — while six Yao have sixty-four possible permutations. Although a thorough study of the sixty-four hexagrams of the I Ching is a specialized field of study, a basic familiarity with the eight trigrams was considered to be common knowledge, especially as they were, and in some cases still are, synonymous with the points of the compass. (Unfortunately, as will be explained below, there are two different correlations of the trigrams with the compass points.)

The I Ching (易經) (regarded as one of the most important of the Chinese classics) was the last of three books written on the interpretation of the Kua. Modern scholarship now accepts that although it was founded on ancient traditions, it was probably written shortly after the death of Confucius, and that the frequently repeated quotation from the Analects (the Sayings of Confucius), that if he had had more years added to his life, he would have spent them all studying the I Ching, is probably a later interpolation. It is not impossible, however, that the period of the I Ching's compilation overlapped the last years of Confucius, which is entirely in accordance with his expressing a wish to have studied it longer. The three books on the Kua were the Lien Shan (連山), the Kuei Tsang (歸藏) and the Chou I, now known as the I Ching. (The titles of the two, older, lost books are usually translated into the most extraordinarily florid and fanciful language, owing to the fact that whereas the meaning is apparent, it is difficult to find English words which can express the Chinese characters with the same degree of laconic terseness. I offer 'Mountain Chains' and 'Return to the Life-Source', but since these two classics are no longer extant the matter is merely academic.)

The aspect of the Kua which is of greatest significance with regards to Mah Jongg is of course the alignment of the eight Kua with the points of the compass. As has been mentioned above, there are two traditionally accepted alignments; the 'ancient' one was attributed to the legendary Fu Hsi, to whom they were revealed on the back of a tortoise (in the same manner, it will be recalled, that the Lo Shu diagram was manifested). The other arrangement in the Great Appendix to the I Ching is attributed to King Wen of the Chou Dynasty (the origin of the I Ching's older title, Chou I). The more ancient Fu Hsi arrangement is much more logical than the one of King Wen. In the Fu Hsi, North is indicated by the central Yao being broken, that is, Yin or 'weak'. Conversely, the Southern points are shown by Kua, which have the central Yao unbroken, hence, Yang or strong. The West Kua has the bottom Yao Yin, the East Kua Yang. With this formula, it is possible to construct the lower two Yao of the Kua for North-East, North-West, South-East, and South-West. The final piece of information, which leads to a construction of all eight Kua, is that in the Kua of the cardinal points, North, East, South, and West, the top Yao is the same as the bottom Yao. This produces all eight compass points. Readers who are familiar with the I Ching will see, if they compare the two arrangements of Fu Hsi and King Wen, that no logical scheme such as the above accounts for the arrangement of Yao in the King Wen scheme.

It was the South, not the North, that was considered by the Chinese to be the principal point of the compass. It was in the South that the Sun made its journey across the Heavens; it was towards the South that the Emperor's doors faced. Lesser mortals' doors faced North. South, according to Fu Hsi, was therefore Yang, and the North Yin. In the same way, because the Sun rose in the East and set in the West, the East was Yang and the West Yin.

The relationship between the compass points, the Kua, and their literal and secondary meanings are shown in the Table on page 47. The reader is advised to study it carefully, bearing in mind that in Mah Jongg East is the dealer's position.

Kua	Compass Point (Fu Hsi)	Chinese	Romanization	Meaning	Interpretation	Yin, Yang	I Ching Name
☰	S	(乾)	Ch'ien	Heaven, Male	Being; Strength; Growth; Continuation Father; Employers; King	⚊	Heaven
☱	SE	(兌)	Tui	Exchange	Reflections; Exchanges; Serenity; Extinguishing; Enchantresses	⚋	Sea
☲	E	(離)	Li	Brightness, Division	Weaponry; Fire; Drought; Ignition; Amazons	⚋	Lightning
☳	NE	(震)	Chen	To Animate	Movement; Travel; Stimulation; Enlivening; Young Men	⚋	Thunder
☷	N	(坤)	K'un	Earth, Female	Docility; Reception; Acceptance; Nourishment; Repose; Subjects; Employees	⚋	Earth
☶	NW	(艮)	Ken	Perverse, Obstinate	Fruition; Maintenance of position; Stability; Places; Custodians; Officials	⚊	Mountain
☵	W	(坎)	K'an	Water-filled pit	Danger; Mental agitation; Instability; Thieves	⚋	Lake
☴	SW	(巽)	Sun	Mildness	Steady Growth; Continuation; Temperance; Trade; Merchants	⚋	Wind

北

N

西北

NW

東北

NE

西 W

E 東

SW

SE

西南

S

南

東南

(iii) Lucky and Unlucky Numbers

While many of the numbers have specific associations — the Five Elements, the Eight Trigrams, the Nine Rivers — there seems to be no regular tradition of lucky and unlucky numbers. I compared two fortune-telling manuals of ancient origin (The Book of Indications of the Great Yellow Genie, and the Book of Indications of the Ruler of the Sacred Barrier) but could see no agreement between them on lucky or unlucky numbers. The two books allocated the equivalent of a five-point scale to the auspiciousness or otherwise of the numbers 1 to 100. The Yellow Genie book was particularly sparing in the allocation of a Very Good rating, which was to the numbers 1, 73, and 91. The Ruler of the Sacred Barrier, however, awarded this accolade to ten numbers, but countered this optimistic slant by designating no less than twenty-seven numbers as Very Unlucky, compared with the Yellow Genie's mere eighteen. Yet only once did these two authorities agree on an extreme rating, both deeming 1 to be Very Lucky. Occasionally, where one authority had an extreme rating, the other would concede to an extent — a number deemed Very Unlucky by one might be considered Rather Unlucky by the other. Unhappily, the agreements were outweighed by the disagreements; in respect of the numbers 8, 65, and 73 (the latter being one of the only three numbers to be deemed Very Lucky by the Yellow Genie) there are diametrically opposing views. Where there is total agreement (apart from the unique case of 1 being thought by both to be Very Lucky) the ratings have always been in the fair to middling category.

My conclusion, therefore, was that there was no tradition of particularly lucky or unlucky numbers, as is the case in the West with respect to 7 and 13.

(iv) Magic Squares

A magic square, mathematically speaking, is a series of numbers written in as many rows as there are figures in each row, and so constructed that the sums of the figures in each row, both horizontally and vertically, add up to the same total. They were regarded as having magical properties and were frequently used as talismans. Examples of magic squares can be found in Arabian, Indian, Greek and other cultures. The Chinese may have been the first to be fascinated by the intricate permutations of numbers that occur in the magic square, for what could be the oldest known representation of a magic square, the Lo Shu (洛書) (Book of the River Lo) occurs in the Great Appendix to the I Ching. In this instance the numbers are indicated, significantly, by spots, as on a domino or dice, the Yang numbers, representing Heaven, being marked as white spots, and the Yin numbers, representing Earth, being marked in black. The I Ching Great Appendix also includes a representation of another series of numbers called the Ho T'u (河圖) (River Picture), similarly delineated.

That these diagrams were considered ancient when the appendix was written is evidenced by the myth describing their origins. According to the legend, the two magic squares were discovered by the Emperor Yü inscribed on the backs of two creatures which emerged from the river on which the emperor had built embankments. The Lo Shu appeared written on the back of a tortoise, and the Ho T'u in green on the back of a dragon-horse. As fantastical as the myths may sound, it is possible that there was a tortoise-shell with flecks on it which might have been interpreted as the spots in the Lo Shu diagram, and that similarly, a reptile or amphibian had a skin with green markings. The point here is the antiquity of the legend, which was known to Confucius (551-478 B.C.): 'The river gives forth no more diagrams' he mourns, in the Lun Yü (Conversations and Discourses). In the West, magic squares were first described by Theon of Smyrna in the second century A.D., but without further mention until more than a thousand years later, when there was a sudden upsurge of interest by Arabic and Byzantine writers in the mathematical and mystical properties of magic squares.

By far the most elegant series of magic squares ever described is the series upon which the 'suit' tiles of the Mah Jongg are built. These squares are the key that unlocks many perplexing questions concerning

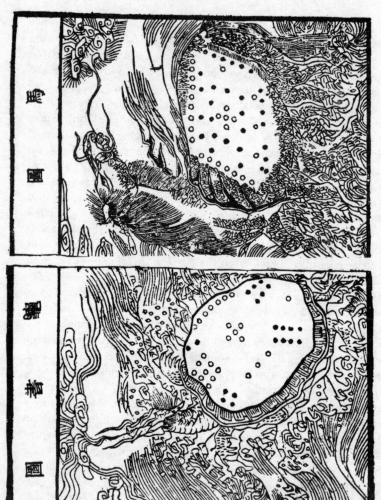

Figure 15. The Lo Shu and Ho T'u.

the Mah Jongg suit tiles: Why there are three suits instead of four? Why there are nine tiles to each suit, instead of ten or twelve? Why do Five Circles play such an important role in certain versions of the game? Is Mah Jongg a Chinese variant of a Western game, or does it have a tradition and history of its own? The elaborate complexities of the magic squares, which result from there being just twenty-seven tiles in the suits and which could result from no other arrangement, show that the Mah Jongg was not put together by chance, or on the spur of the moment. It exhibits such symmetry and perfection of form that it could only have evolved out of a tradition steeped in a profound appreciation of the mystical powers of numbers.

Imagine one each of the suit tiles — twenty-seven in all — being placed in a stack, three layers high, each of three rows of three tiles. The number of possible permutations in which the tiles could be arranged is staggering: 18 followed by twenty-six more digits. We shall, however, consider only one such arrangement, the one shown in the illustration.

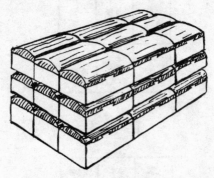

Figure 16. The 27 Mah Jongg suit tiles, stacked in three layers of three rows.

The following relationships emerge. The top layer is a magic square thus:

$$\begin{array}{ccc} 2 & 4 & 9 \\ 7 & 3 & 5 \\ 6 & 8 & 1 \end{array}$$

It will be seen that each row, vertically and horizontally, adds up to 15. The central layer is also a magic square; in fact the Lo Shu of the I Ching. (This magic square, however, has the additional property in that its diagonals also add up to 15.) Similarly, the lowest layer forms another magic square.

列下

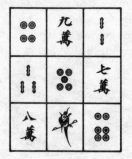

書洛

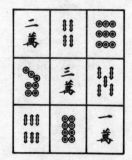

列上

Figure 17. The three layers of the Mah Jongg suit tiles, with the Lo Shu magic square in the centre.

If the stack is viewed from the side, then another square of tiles is seen, made from the left hand rank of each layer, or the front or back row of each layer, giving another four squares altogether. Each of these is a magic square as well. Then there are the squares formed by taking the central slice out of the stack, either front to back or side to side. These too are magic squares, but are squares of the Lo Shu type, in which the diagonals as well add up to 15. In addition, any row which goes from one corner of the stack, passing through the central Five Circles to the opposite corner, also adds up to 15.

But this is only the warm-up to a truly remarkable phenomenon. If the tiles are numbered from one to twenty-seven, beginning with 1 bamboo, through the circle suits, and ending with 9 wan, an entirely new set of magic squares is generated. **Every single row throughout the stack, vertically or horizontally, and every row which passes through the central tile of 5 circles (number 14 in the series) adds up to 42.** Compared with the magic squares of the Arabian talismans, the Mah Jongg mathematical arrangement is a nuclear pile.

THE MAH JONGG TILES, AS NUMBERED 1 TO 27

Bamboo	
1	1
2	2
3	3
4	4
5	5
6	6
7	7
8	8
9	9

Circle	
1	10
2	11
3	12
4	13
5	14
6	15
7	16
8	17
9	18

Wan	
1	19
2	20
3	21
4	22
5	23
6	24
7	25
8	26
9	27

THE NUMBERS OF THE THREE LAYERS OF MAGIC SQUARES

20	4	18
16	21	5
6	17	19

13	27	2
3	14	25
26	1	15

9	11	22
23	7	12
10	24	8

（洛書）

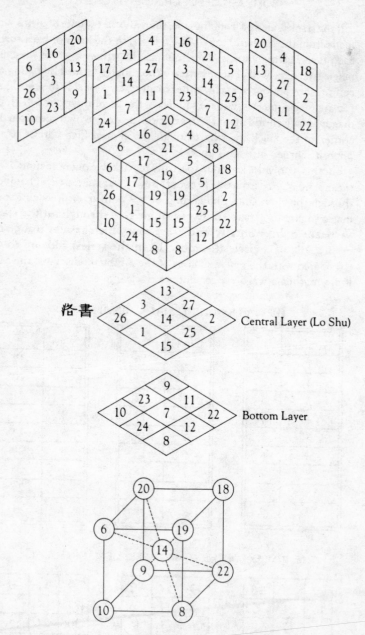

洛書 Central Layer (Lo Shu)

Bottom Layer

Figure 18. A dissection of the principal magic squares in the Mah Jongg stack of 27 suit tiles.

(v) The Chinese Written Language

All forms of divination are basically signs or portents interpreted by a reader, who supplements the primary significance of the oracle with his own subjective versions of the symbolism. Just how much the oracle is embroidered by the reader depends very much on the nature of the question, the degree of ambiguity of the oracle, and the imagination of the reader. It makes little difference whether the oracle is a star chart, a number drawn by lots, a dream, tea leaves, or the palm of the hand. Those who consult astrologers expect to have more than a birth chart, no matter how painstakingly accurate it may have been drawn up. Advice, interpretations, and predictions are what the client has come for. The reputation of a particular oracle depends less on its communications than on the power of the soothsayer to interpret them.

In this respect, a mastery of the Chinese written language lays the foundation of imaginative and interpretative skill, since Chinese characters often have to convey abstract ideas by the presentation of concrete ones. It is not suggested that anyone wishing to develop the art of Mah Jongg divination will have to learn fluent Chinese, or even any Chinese at all. But a few examples of how Chinese script is able to convey different ideas will give a good idea of how juxtapositions of different Mah Jongg tiles might lend themselves to interpretation.

Some Chinese characters are obvious picture signs, such as (大) a man with his arms outstretched for 'big' or 'great', or the delightfully descriptive (傘) for 'umbrella'. Others use a concrete idea to convey an abstract one, as in (易), the I of I Ching. This was originally meant to represent a chameleon, which could change its colour — hence the sign meant 'change'. (言) is a picture of a mouth with something issuing from it — that is to say, speech, or a word. A man's word is another way of saying 'promise', so the sign for a man together with that of word makes the character for 'promise' (信). Even with just a few elements it is possible to construct several ideas. Take the following: (亻) man, (女) girl, (宀) roof, (囗) pen, (豕) pig. A pig in a pen (圂) makes a 'pigsty', a man in a pen is a 'prisoner' (囚). A cottage, therefore a home, and by extension a 'family', is shown by a pig under a roof: (家). A man about the home would be useful making 'furniture': (傢); when a girl thinks of home and family she thinks of 'marriage': (嫁); a girl on her own under a roof (安) indicates 'peace and tranquility'; but two girls together (姦) could mean 'intrigue'. One man following another (从) shows 'obedience'. Five simple characters have generated eight more.

Although on occasions the relative positions of the elements in a character makes no difference to the meaning or pronunciation (as in

(棋) or (棊), Ch'i, a gaming piece), usually a change of position indicates both a difference in meaning and pronunciation. An excellent example can be shown with the characters for tree (木) and Sun (日). The sun above the trees (杲) indicates brightness, and conversely the sun below the trees (杳) means obscurity; while (東), the rising sun behind the trees, indicates the East.

Juggling such ideas about the ancient Chinese devised an entire vocabulary of symbols. They too, might nod occasionally, and create a new character for a word when one already existed. Even Confucius complained of scribes who were too lazy to look up a character they had forgotten, and instead of leaving a blank space filled up the gap with a new sign of their own invention. But the intricacies of the Chinese language need not concern the reader so much as the need to develop the state of mind which can assemble unrelated ideas to create a new thought. There are nearly three million different permutations of three Mah Jongg tiles possible. Little would be gained in listing them all, for by far the greater part of the fascination and stimulation of Mah Jongg divination lies in its seemingly limitless fund of answers which it can supply. Approached with a problem, the Mah Jongg will provide the concepts for the reader to organize a course of action.

[The ruling deity of the constellation Tou.]

PART TWO
Divination by Mah Jongg

3.
READING THE
MAH JONGG TILES

There are different ways of consulting the Mah Jongg tiles; from the elaborate ceremonial of 'Five Steps' to the more hurried decision-making method based on one tile. All methods involve the same initial procedure — placing the tiles face downwards on the table, shuffling them; then pushing thirteen tiles to the centre and reshuffling. It is from the middle of the reshuffled thirteen tiles that one tile — the 'Chung' tile — is taken for a simple answer to a straightforward question. When a more extended reading is wanted, it is important to take into account not only the tiles themselves, but also the tiles which are next to them, and even the position of the tiles in the four rows. The Catalogue of Tiles (p. 73) lists several named combinations, but naturally it is only possible to include a selection as a general guideline.

For the reader who prefers a more visionary approach, the 'Secondary Meanings' of the tiles with their guardians should be stimulating; it is not necessary for the guardian to be present for this Secondary Meaning to be read and interpreted in the light of the questioner's background.

The Commentaries on the symbolism of the tiles end with a few hints on specific problems — romance, business, health and career. These are guidelines based on the symbolism of the tile on its own. The following points are explained in greater detail under their respective headings, but nothing is lost by reiterating them.

Note the tiles which appear in the 'First' and 'Last' places (see the diagram p. 186). These retain their own 'First' tile and 'Last' tile interpretation, even though they may form associations with other tiles.

Examine each row of tiles: see if any pairs or groups of three tiles in any row form doubles or 'associations'. It will be necessary to check the list at the beginning of the 'Catalogue'. Every tile forms at least one association.

Do not transfer tiles from one row to another.

If any tile turned up is a 'Guardian' tile, (Flowers or Seasons) take another tile: usually the nearest in the remaining pool.

Most Mah Jongg sets available on the market today consist of 144 tiles, but some variations are to be expected, especially in Japanese and American sets. These may contain an extra four blanks to replace any which get mislaid, and such blanks can merely be put to one side. Unfortunately, some sets, intended specifically for playing, lack the Eight Guardians. This does not rule out the use of such sets as a vehicle for Mah Jongg divination, but obviously the sets which include the Guardians are to be preferred. On the other hand, there are some sets, especially of the older variety, which have more Guardian tiles. These are described below.

Apart from these eight guardian tiles (Seasons and Flowers) the rest of the Mah Jongg set consists of four identical 'packs' of thirty-four tiles each. Each 'pack' has three suits — Bamboo, Circles, and Wan (Ten Thousands) numbered from 1 to 9; four 'compass points' (East, South, West, North) and three tiles known to English speakers as 'Dragons' (although we shall see that they are no such thing), two of which are marked with Chinese characters, and one blank.

Further comments on the Mah Jongg tiles and their symbolism is given below.

(i) The Eight Guardians

The Eight Guardians, sometimes known as 'Flowers' or 'Seasons', are the only tiles in the Mah Jongg set which are not duplicated. They represent the Eight Trigrams of the I Ching, and as such are associated with the eight points of the compass. Each tile is engraved with a rather stylized picture of the flower or season which it represents. The more usual Guardians are the Four Flowers and the Four Seasons of the year. The Four Flowers, known to the Chinese as the Four Nobles, have a special significance in poetry and painting. Each Flower is proper to a particular season, and each Season with a point of the compass, as explained in the table.

Somewhat rarer are the Guardians Wind, Flower, Snow, and Moon, and the Four Sages, Fisher, Woodcutter, Farmer, and Scholar. These are used exactly as the Season or Flower Guardians which they replace.

THE GUARDIAN TILES AND THEIR RELATIONSHIPS

Kua	Tile	Related Compass Point	Alternative Guardian Tiles	
䷝ Li	(李) Plum Blossom	North East	Yü (魚) Fisherman	Feng (風) Wind
䷖ Ch'un	(春) Spring	East (東) Tung		
䷳ Lan	(蘭) Orchid	South East	Ch'iao (樵) Woodcutter	Hua (華) Flower
䷞ Hsia	(夏) Summer	South (南) Nan		
䷵ Chü	(菊) Chrysanthemum	South West	Keng (耕) Farmer	Hsüeh (雪) Snow
䷃ Ch'iu	(秋) Autumn	West (西) Hsi		
䷲ Chu	(竹) Bamboo	North West	Tu (讀) Scholar	Yüeh (月) Moon
䷇ Tung	(冬) Winter	North (北) Pei		

(ii) The Four Directions

The four points of the compass are engraved in black in Chinese characters viz: Tung (東) East; Nan (南) South; Hsi (西) West; Pei (北) North. The Chinese word for East, Tung, also has connotations of leadership and authority (because the Sun rises in the East). In Mah Jongg games, the player who is East always plays first off, and acts as dealer. In older Mah Jongg sets, East was shown by tiles signifying the highest order of nobility.

It is important to stress that the Chinese formerly held that there were five (not four) cardinal points, the fifth being Chung, or Centre (中). In modern Mah Jongg sets this tile is marked in red, but it may be recalled that in one of the earliest Mah Jongg-like games ever recorded (see Part 1, p. 41) the Chung tile was marked in black, like the other cardinal point tiles.

(iii) The Three Extremes

There are three tiles which are known to English-speaking players as the Three 'Dragons'. They are not so known in Chinese, and it is misleading to refer to them as such. There is one tile which properly should be blank, but which is sometimes distinguished from the spare blanks either by having a frame engraved on it, or else the letter 'P' (for Pai, white) or even the word 'White'. The other two tiles are marked with the Chinese characters Fa (發) (in green) and Chung (中) (in red). English players, probably because they do not know the meaning of the Chinese characters, usually call these tiles by the colour, red, green, or white, and add the oriental-sounding 'dragon' to give the name some authenticity. The actual meaning of the Chinese characters is: Fa, (發) to give out, issue, or commence, and referred to in this manual as 'Beginning'; Chung, (中) middle, centre, or to catch, and known in this manual as 'Centre'; Pai, (白) white, pure, absence, known here as 'White'.

(iv) The Suit Tiles

The suits originally represented values, of which Bamboos were the lowest, Circles the central rank, and the 'character' suit the highest. In old sets, the Bamboo tiles were marked with rectangles. The Circle tiles, known as T'ung, written (筒) but which more properly should be (銅), represented copper coins. The tiles marked with Chinese characters are in fact the Ten Thousands, from 10,000 to 90,000. Such tiles usually have the Arabic equivalents of the numbers engraved on them, but for those who only have a set marked with Chinese numerals, the Arabic equivalents are as follows:

(一) (二) (三) (四) (五) (六) (七) (八) (九)
 1   2   3   4   5   6   7   8   9

The word for ten thousand (it is convenient to resurrect the old word 'myriad' for an accurate translation) is Wan, which may be written either (萬) or (万), and both forms can be found on different makes of Mah Jongg tiles. Like the word 'myriad', Wan is also used in the sense of a great, if indefinite, number.

(v) The Colours of the Tiles

Mah Jongg tiles are usually engraved in three colours: red, green and black (or blue). *Those who possess sets marked in blue as one of the colours should read 'blue' for 'black' throughout the rest of this section.* All the Wan tiles are engraved in two colours, red and black, and are therefore said to be 'impure'. The Bamboo tiles are predominantly green, the Circle tiles a variety of combinations of black, green and red. Tiles marked in three colours are 'perfect', those marked in two colours 'impure', and those in one colour are 'pure'.

(vi) The Names and Meanings of the Tiles

The following is a table of the suit tiles, together with their colours, and the names by which each tile is known in Mah Jongg divination.

1 Bamboo	Peacock	red, green, black	perfect
2 Bamboo	Duck	green	pure
3 Bamboo	Toad	green	pure
4 Bamboo	Carp	green	pure
5 Bamboo	Lotus	green, red	impure
6 Bamboo	Water	green	pure
7 Bamboo	Tortoise	red, green, black	perfect
8 Bamboo	Mushrooms	green	pure
9 Bamboo	Willow-Tree (or Nine Virtues)	green, red	impure
1 Circle	Pearl (Moon)	red, green, black	perfect
2 Circles	Pine	black, green	impure
3 Circles	Phoenix	red, green, black	perfect
4 Circles	Jade	black, green	impure
5 Circles	Dragon	red, green, black	perfect
6 Circles	Peach	red, black	impure
7 Circles	Insect	red, black	impure
8 Circles	Tiger	black	pure
9 Circles	Unicorn	red, green, black	perfect
1 Wan	Entering	red, black	impure
2 Wan	Double-edged sword	red, black	impure
3 Wan	Earth	red, black	impure
4 Wan	Lute	red, black	impure
5 Wan	House	red, black	impure
6 Wan	Fire	red, black	impure
7 Wan	Stars	red, black	impure
8 Wan	Knot	red, black	impure
9 Wan	Heaven	red, black	impure

The 1 Bamboo is nowadays invariably marked with a design of some stylized bird, sometimes called a 'rice-bird'. 7 Bamboo (Tortoise), 3 Circle (Phoenix, 5 Circles (Dragon), and 9 Circles (Unicorn), are collectively known as the Four (Fabulous) Beasts.

(vii) Associations

It will be seen from the above table that tiles marked in three colours are called 'perfect', those in two colours 'impure' and those in one colour, 'pure'. It is not necessary to learn which tiles have which colours, unless the set from which you are working happens to be a cheaper version without the colours. Otherwise, whether the tiles are perfect, impure or pure is apparent immediately on looking at the tile. When an impure tile is joined with a pure tile of the third colour it forms a perfect association. Any of the Wan tiles will therefore form a perfect association with any of the pure (green) Bamboo tiles or Beginning (Fa, the 'Green Dragon'). However, certain associations of the Wan tiles with particular green tiles are of especial importance. These are known as the Nine Felicitous Associations, and are of particularly good portent. These are listed in the Summary Index which preceeds the Catalogue of Tiles (p. 73).

In addition to the Nine Felicitous Associations there are Five Harmonious Associations. A glance at the above table will show that there are six pure green tiles, five pure black tiles (the Four Cardinal Points, and 8 Circles, Tiger) and only one pure red tile, Chung, Centre. Of the many possible perfect associations which can be formed between these pure tiles and the impure ones, five are of especial importance, and indicate the change of a malign influence into a beneficial one.

FIVE HARMONIOUS ASSOCIATIONS

North and 9 Bamboo (Willow-tree) ....Strength
8 Circles (Tiger) and 5 Bamboo (Lotus).........................Wisdom
Chung (Centre) and 4 Circles (Jade).............................Esteem
Chung (Centre) and 2 Circles (Pine) ....Peace
6 Bamboo (Water) and 6 Circles (Peach) ....Health

The White Tile

The White tile is both pure and perfect, and may be conjoined to any group of tiles without affecting their associations.

Perfect Tiles

Perfect tiles may join to any association of tiles that is already perfect; the association will still be perfect. If a perfect tile is added to a pure tile, the association is mutually enhancing; the perfection of one tile enhances the purity of the other, while the purity of the latter enhances the perfection of the first. Each retains its own purity or perfection; they do

not lose their original identity as in the Nine Felicitous or Five
Harmonious associations. The exception is the White tile, whose purity
is absorbed by the perfect tile.

A perfect tile may be associated with an imperfect tile or pair of tiles.
The tiles remain imperfect, apart from four special cases, which is when
the perfect tile is one of the Four Fabulous Beasts.

The Four Fabulous Beasts
The Four Fabulous Beasts — Tortoise (7 Bamboo); Phoenix (3 Circles);
Dragon (5 Circles); and Unicorn (9 Circles) — are said to be *in their realms*
when in association with the following tiles:

Tortoise, (7 Bamboo)	realm is . . . North	Memory
Phoenix, (3 Circles)	realm is . . . South	Prosperity
Dragon, (5 Circles)	realm is . . . East	Benevolence
Unicorn, (9 Circles)	realm is . . . West, or White	Nobility

When the beasts are in their realms, the Cardinal Points proper to the
beasts become white, and consequently pure and perfect.

Associations of Three Tiles
Associations of three tiles may be perfect, if their colours are
harmoniously proportioned. The following associations are perfect if
there is one tile from each pair:

5 Bamboo (Lotus)	2 Circles (Pine)	6 Circles (Peach)
(green and red)	*(black and green)*	*(black and red)*
9 Bamboo (Willow)	4 Circles (Jade)	7 Circles (Insect)

There are thus eight such associations possible, of which two have
special significance. These are:

9 Bamboo (Willow)	2 Circles (Pine and	
	6 Circles (Peach)	Three Trees
5 Bamboo (Lotus)	4 Circles (Jade) and	
	7 Circles (Insect)	Treasure

Of course, the eight associations can be extended by including any of the
black and red Wan tiles, but the list would become so numerous that it
would be beyond the scope of this guide to list them.

Associations of Three Pure Tiles

Three pure tiles, one of each colour, make a perfect association. As has already been pointed out, there are six pure green tiles, five pure black tiles and one pure red tile. There are thirty such associations possible, but only one has prime significance. This is 4 Bamboo (Carp), 8 Circles (Tiger) and Chung (Centre), which is called *Valour*.

The white tile has the power to take on the value of any colour, when with two pure tiles of different colours. Thus, perfect associations may be formed by Centre, Tiger, and White, which has otherwise no green tile; or by West, Water and White, which has no red tile. Only one association is of prime significance, but it is the most important of all: it is Fa (Beginning), Chung (Middle, in this context) and White (End) and is called *Eternity*.

The Significance of the Colours

Generally speaking, the symbolism of the four colours is that green represents vegetative life; red, animal life; black, earthly or inanimate things; and white, spiritual beings.

4.

INTERPRETING THE TILES

A glance at the names of the suit tiles will show that for the most part they bear the names of things. They may be creatures, real or mythical, such as the Tiger, Duck, Unicorn or Phoenix; some of them are plants, such as Willow, Lotus, and Pine; and one or two are objects, like the Lute, House, or Water. The tiles, as well as having a Common Name, also have an Attribute name, which is its Greater Meaning. These are generally speaking the names of emotions, and abstract concepts. Thirdly, it has a lesser, or commonplace meaning, for immediate, rather than philosophical, consideration.

After a brief discussion of the various meanings of the tile, there follows a summary of its more important associations. By far the most important of these is its association with its own Guardian tile. This will often radically alter the meaning of the tile, and in any case, a special name pertains to all pairs formed between a tile and its proper Guardian. Each suit tile has therefore a secondary Common Name, and secondary Greater and Lesser Meanings. It is important to stress that when a suit tile appears with its proper Guardian, it is to be regarded as an altogether separate tile. When a tile forms an association with another tile on account of the colours being harmonious, and one of the tiles has a proper Guardian, neither of the tiles forming the association will have its original meaning: the one with its proper Guardian will become a 'new tile' with a new meaning and concept, and the tile without the Guardian will lose its identity in the association of the two tiles.

The Guardians themselves generally have no meaning of their own. The important exceptions are when they are guarding a white tile. This tile, Purity, serves to enhance the meaning of the Guardian, and in this case the interpretation is that of the Guardian. The other important exceptions are when the Guardians appear as the Chung, First or Last tiles. The Chung tile is the one in the Centre of the spread; at the central cardinal point. Like all the other tiles, the Guardians reveal a specific 'lesser' meaning at the Chung (Centre) Cardinal Point. Similarly, emphasis is placed on those tiles which appear as the first tile of the East position, and the last tile of the North position, such tiles being called the First and Last tiles.

Associations

It has already been shown that certain pairs of tiles form an association of a named kind — Felicitous Associations, Beasts in their Realms, and so on. Many other associations are possible, not all of them of good portent. The more striking of these are listed under the specific tiles, but as has already been pointed out, it would require a massive volume to catalogue all the possible associations between the tiles.

The Order of the Tiles in the Catalogue

The interpretations appear in the following order:

Firstly, the Four Nobles, (the flowers) and the Four Seasons.

Secondly, the Three Extremes, ('Dragons' or 'Colours') Fa, Chung, and Pai, followed by the Four Cardinal Points, East, South, West and North.

Thirdly, the Three Suits, Bamboo, Circles, and Wan, in that order.

The interpretations of pairs and other sets of tiles are given under their first appearance in the catalogue; thus 8 Bamboo and 5 Wan with West is listed under its first appearance at West.

The Cardinal Points

The Chinese, as previously noted, considered there to be five cardinal points; not just East, South, West and North, but Centre as well. This was because the Cardinals were not considered to be directions so much as areas. Chung-Kuo, China, was the Middle Kingdom, and the rest of the world stood in relation to it.

The four black tiles which form the outer cardinal points obviously bear harmonious relationship to those areas on the table which are called by the compass points. These areas have a tentative function with regard to time and place, and since the cardinal points are shortly to be discussed more fully with regards to the tiles and associations they form, it might be worthwhile at this point to look at the Cardinal Areas in more detail.

In the East

Those tiles which are immediately in front of the reader pertain to the questioner, his immediate present and his surroundings. The tiles at that point bear relevance to what he is doing at the current time, assuming that he is consulting the Mah Jongg Oracle with a view to looking at any changes which may have to be made in his thinking.

In the South and North

The South and North sectors refer to the questioner's immediate past and future, but not necessarily separately. Very broadly speaking, the South represents immediate past and the North immediate future, but this rule is so general as not to be accurate at all. In another way, it might be said that the South sector shows the good influences at work, and the North the dangers or bad influences. Furthermore, South very often indicates travel possibilities, while North represents the results of non-action. South is Yang and North is Yin. Then again, the last tile, the North's third, is always taken to be the end result, which might point to the North being distant future and the South immediate future. (However, this is not a hard and fast rule, as will be seen from the commentaries on the tiles.)

In the West

The West sector represents those things which are either furthest from the questioner, or in opposition. Tiles in the West sector might therefore show events which are happening somewhere else but which will have a bearing on the questioner later on. They are those things which are outside his present knowledge, whereas the East deals with those things of which he has a relationship at the moment. The West may also represent people who work in opposition to the questioner; or those forces which might impede his work; or even, the work itself, if it is in the nature of the questioner's work for it to be an obstacle to him. If the questioner is a marketer, then the East may represent the things which he markets, and the West the field into which he has to place his merchandise. West in general represents the objective side, whereas the East is the subjective one.

One curious feature regarding Mah Jongg in connection with the points of the compass, is that the terms East, West, North and South do not correspond to the order of the cardinal points on a map and compass. North is to the left of East, South to the right. The reason is complex and ties up with astrological traditions.

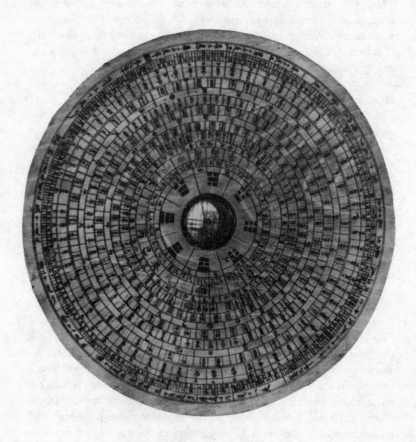

Geomancer's Compass (see p. 29).

SUMMARY INDEX TO THE CATALOGUE OF TILES

Bamboo		120
1 Bamboo	Peacock	121
1 Bamboo, 1 Circle	Vanity	122
2 Bamboo	Duck	123
2 Bamboo, 2 Wan	Companionship	124
3 Bamboo	Toad	124
3 Bamboo, 8 Wan	Discovery	126
4 Bamboo	Carp	126
4 Bamboo, 8 Circles, Centre	*(Valour)*	100
4 Bamboo, 4 Wan	Reconciliation	128
4 Bamboo, 7 Wan	Reward	128
5 Bamboo	Lotus	128
5 Bamboo, 4 Circles, 7 Circles	Treasure	130
5 Bamboo, 8 Circles	Wisdom	130
6 Bamboo	Water	130
6 Bamboo, 6 Circles	Health	132
6 Bamboo, 3 Wan	Abundance	132
6 Bamboo, 6 Wan	Progress	132
7 Bamboo	Tortoise	133
7 Bamboo-North	*(Memory)*	118
8 Bamboo	Mushrooms	134
8 Bamboo, 5 Wan	Knowledge	136
9 Bamboo	Willow-tree	136
9 Bamboo-North	*(Strength)*	119
9 Bamboo, 2 Circles, 6 Circles	Three Trees	137
Circles		138
1 Circle	Pearl (Moon)	139
1 Circle, 1 Bamboo	*(Vanity)*	122
2 Circles	Pine	141
2 Circles, Centre	*(Peace)*	101
2 Circles, 9 Bamboo, 6 Circles	*(Three Trees)*	137
3 Circles	Phoenix	142
3 Circles-South	*(Prosperity)*	113
4 Circles	Jade	144
4 Circles-Centre	*(Esteem)*	102
4 Circles, 5 Bamboo, 7 Circles	*(Treasure)*	130
5 Circles	Dragon	146
5 Circles-East	*(Benevolence)*	110

CATALOGUE OF TILES

李　蘭　菊　竹

(i) THE FOUR NOBLES

The four Flower tiles, Plum, Orchid, Chrysanthemum and Bamboo, have been regarded since time immemorial by the Chinese as the Four Nobles. In painting, the highest ideal to which one could aspire was to depict one of the Four Nobles in perfection. Even their very contemplation would inspire numerous poems, and in introducing the mention of one of the Four Nobles a Chinese sage would convey more to his listener than a paragraph of words, since his scholar would be fully aware of the deep symbolism inherent in the perfection of the plant's nature.

The reader might do well to consider for a few moments the different nature of these four plants. Apart from their appropriateness to the four seasons, there are the significant differences of detail. Each plant is of a contrasting type. The plum is a tree, bearing welcome blossom in the spring and delicious fruit in the summer, while the orchid is a small and delicate flower, rare and beautiful, inhabiting tiny crevices in rocks and trees. It was, more particularly, esteemed for its exquisite perfume. Quite different again is the splendid chrysanthemum, appreciated for its symmetry, magnificence, and appearance when the flowers of summer were fading. Lastly, bamboo, evergreen and grasslike, not only had an intrinsic beauty of its own; it was an economic plant upon which Chinese domestic life depended.

Being plants, all the flowers harmonize with Fa (發) Beginning, (the green character tile) and like the four seasons, display their full nature in association with Pai (白) White. Unlike the Four Seasons, the Four Nobles represent the pursuit of leisure, ideals and beauty — the four seasons being concerned more with work and the necessities of everyday life. The four scholarly pursuits (also represented by the tile 4 Wan) are painting, poetry, chess and music, although no particular flower is associated with each of these pursuits. With regard to the principle of Yin and Yang, the Four Nobles are collectively Yin, and therefore feminine and receptive.

PLUM (Also known as **THE FISHERMAN**)

(Li) 李

YOUTHFUL OPTIMISM — FRIENDSHIP

Agrees with: Ch'un (春) Spring   Fa (發) Beginning
                 Tung (東) East   Pai (白) White

Proper Guardian of: 1 Bamboo, Peacock
                      4 Circles, Unicorn
                      1 Wan, Entering

Commentary

> Though the apricot is not in blossom
> Yet crimson petals flutter from the plum tree.

The pink blossoms of the plum are a delight after the bareness of the winter trees, heralding warmer and happier times. The fresh and pretty blossoms are, however, short lived and soon blown down by the boisterous spring winds. The mature fruits are gathered as leaves begin to fall; the first hints of winter are on their way.

The symbolism is of youthful optimism, inexperience and innocence; all the delights and pleasures, but the pains as well, of youth. Inexperience and youthful optimism has to come face to face eventually with the harshness of reality, and the sometimes cruel consequences. Since the plum is not an autumn sign, it does not represent the rewards of harvest, but rather the inevitability of time passing, and is a caution against caprice.

Chung tile: There will be great success very quickly. Good news will come soon.

First tile: Happiness and lightheartedness. A joyous occasion shortly. If with a green tile, a love affair outside one's normal relationships; a chance but brief encounter.

Last tile: Opportunities will arise which you may grasp, but be prepared to face the consequences realistically.

With the Pai (White) tile:

In the East: East being harmonious with Plum, the dangers of youthful folly are minimized. Here are the pleasures and pastimes of youth without the pessimism of experience. Pleasant encounters, friendships, and affairs of the heart.

In the South: Summer winds fan chance meetings into longer lasting romances. Friendships are more mature, if less ecstatic. There is an indication of shared joys, especially with regards to the sharing of cultural pursuits, such as visits to the theatre, concerts and so on.

In the West: Here are the warnings of older people; pessimism and perhaps disenchantment. One is left clutching a faded flower. Do not put too much reliance on things which are transient.

In the North: Sudden gusts of wind shake the plum-laden trees, scattering the fruit to the ground and bruising them. The hurts and regrets of one's mistakes are harder than those done by other people. But hope will always conquer disillusionment, and another spring is not so far away.

Also see references under 1 Bamboo and 5 Circles.

———————————— • ————————————

ORCHID (Also known as the **WOODCUTTER**)   (Lan)

LOVE — BEAUTY — ELEGANCE — REFINEMENT — CHARM — JOY

Agrees with: Hsia (夏) Summer   Fa (發) Beginning (Green)
                 Pai (白) White   Nan (南) South

Proper Guardian of: 4 Bamboo, Carp
                     1 Circle, Pearl
                     4 Wan, Lute
                     7 Wan, Stars

Commentary

The orchid is a sign of luxury, but not in the wasteful sense, rather the luxury of fine things, craftsmanship, perfection. The orchid is not only beautiful, but rare, so there is delight in appreciating things not only for their intrinsic beauty but for their precious qualities. In the orchid we see the connoisseur appreciating the finer things, ideals and concepts of life. One can also appreciate things not only for their rarity, but for their exquisite workmanship. Beyond the visual beauty of the orchid is the delicate fragrance for which it was renowned; 'orchid-scented' was an epithet of high esteem. Its redolent perfume symbolizes finer qualities which go further than the qualities of a thing in itself; qualities indefinable and tenuous, but nevertheless apparent to the person of taste.

The orchid blossoms in secret, in remote, inaccessible places, betraying itself only by its perfume. In this sense the orchid may signify someone who is only known by his good works or his reputation; someone who is sought after, rather than someone who actively seeks to make his name.

It signifies the perfect human being, and is the symbol of joy. It betokens craftsmanship, and is the sign of jewellers, woodcarvers, and all who make small works of art.

Chung tile:	You will experience the pleasant enjoyment of success. Refined pleasure.
First tile:	An opportunity to acquire some luxurious thing will present itself, which you would not regret. A person of great beauty and refinement will make your acquaintance, and the memory of the meeting will linger like the orchid's perfume.
Last tile:	The sweetness of the perfume of the orchid can be savoured even though the flower itself is not visible. After a successful effort, the satisfaction will linger.
In the East:	An indication of the appreciation of fine things; something precious and close to you will be appreciated more than usual.
In the South:	There will be movement and joy; there is a sign of a journey of pleasing consequence, or a visit which brings happiness.

In the West: There is quiet refinement. News of something valuable from afar. In business, dealings with foreign countries in small things. In affairs of the heart, a foreign person.

In the North: Something of great value. An object of *vertu*; an antique brooch, a painted miniature, an intricately worked piece, something of which the worth is greater than its face value.

———————— • ————————

CHRYSANTHEMUM (Also known as THE FARMER)   (Chü) 菊

FRIENDS — NOBILITY — RETIREMENT

Agrees with: Ch'iu (秋) Autumn   Fa (發) Beginning (Green)
          Pai (白) White   Hsi (西) West

Proper Guardian of: 7 Circles, Insect
          3 Wan, Earth
          6 Wan, Fire

Commentary

The chrysanthemum appears in the autumn, when the flowers of summer are beginning to disappear; but instead of peeping modestly through the ground like a spring flower it blazes forth in a glory of colour. The colours of chrysanthemums, white, rust and yellow, are the colours of flames as well as the colours of silver, copper and gold. The chrysanthemum's flurry of petals is not like the delicate arrangement of the orchid's.

What a wealth of symbolism there is here! The last of the van, arriving in a splendour of triumph, accounts for it being a symbol of nobility, the sign of the Sun itself; its flame colours associate it with fire, and all that entails — not so much a consuming fire, but fire harnessed to a purpose. For this reason, and for its association with the metal colours, it is the symbol of workers and dealers in metals and, by extension, to men who work in handling coin. The sign of alchemy, in modern times it has become the emblem of industrial chemists.

Its myriad petals indicate fecundity, wealth, and fortune, or any dealings in products on a large scale; wholesalers, or dealers in bulk goods. On the negative side, the chrysanthemum symbolizes the grosser side of man's nature; the love of amassing vast wealth, a concern with quantity rather than quality. Its gaudiness shows up the tawdriness and ostentatiousness of the greedy, the grasping and those with a lack of discernment.

Its late but gorgeous arrival shows a lack of modesty and restraint. It indicates a love of display, self-esteem, and an egotistical nature; it indicates people who are perhaps more concerned with impression rather than depth.

There is another curious aspect of the chrysanthemum. Being a flower of harvest time, it is connected with one of the jollier aspects of that season: wine-making. It therefore also indicates the pleasure of drinking. A charming folk-tale, which was collected by an early Chinese story-teller* from the countryfolk in his region, tells the tale of two chrysanthemum spirits who took human form. One of them was a female spirit who married and enjoyed a long life. The other, however, her brother, was far too fond of drinking. Unfortunately, whenever he drank too much, he would peel off all his clothes and then pass out in the flower bed, where he would change back into a chrysanthemum. The husband finding his brother-in-law undergoing this strange metamorphosis one evening, rushed to his aid but inadvertently killed him.

If one is aware of the negative side of Chrysanthemum, there are still many positive qualities that one can enjoy in moderation. These are the pleasures of companionship, friends, a happy retirement; the enjoyment of the autumn of one's years, or even more specifically the enjoyment of autumn's pleasures; the last heady days of an Indian summer. Chinese poets, long before Omar, had frequently expressed the simple pleasure of getting slightly intoxicated while watching the Sun set behind the hills, and exchanging verses with a revered companion.

Chung tile: The sign of Nobility indicates that an honour of rank will be bestowed.

First tile: There is a sign of great reward, indicated by the colours of the chrysanthemum: silver, copper and gold. It indicates prosperity.

Last tile: The meaning of Chrysanthemum as a last tile is modified by the tiles with it in the North; it may

*Pu Sung-Ling

mean a happy retirement, accumulation of wealth, or contentment with friends. With North or West wind, however, it has the significance 'strivings after riches'.

In the East: Chrysanthemum being the guardian of the White tile in the East shows wealth, or public honour.

In the South: Pleasurable enjoyment; happiness and companionship with old friends. Merrymaking. In business, the sign is one of gain.

In the West: The chrysanthemum takes on some of its less favourable aspects if associated with negative tiles. Great display; much wealth. High living, high society. Public acknowledgement, fame. Guard against future disappointments.

In the North: Generally, the negative side of Chrysanthemum is heightened in the North; the presence of other tiles will indicate the dangers. It can mean loss, disappointment. In business, guard against too speculative ventures. In affairs of the heart, beware of people who lack sincerity.

———————— ● ————————

BAMBOO (Also known as THE SCHOLAR)   (Chu) 竹

VIRTUE — CONSTANCY — FRIENDSHIP EVEN IN ADVERSITY

Agrees with: Tung (冬) Winter   Fa (發) Beginning (Green)
Pai (白) White   Pei (北) North

Proper Guardian of: 3 Bamboo, Toad
6 Bamboo, Water
9 Bamboo, Willow
4 Circles, Jade

Commentary
The Bamboo has always been highly regarded in China, not only for its

elegance, but also for its utility. It was considered to enshrine all the attributes which were the Chinese ideals of perfect manhood. Its physical characteristics, uprightness, straight growth and regularly spaced knots, were a symbol of manly physique; the elegantly long and green leaves, freshly green even in winter, symbolized purity and clarity in thought and action. Its firmness and strength were those of determination; its evergreen qualities showed endurance; it survived the ice and snow of winter, yet in the face of fierce gales it was able to bend and give way without being destroyed. Its flexibility enabled it to withstand the onslaught of ice, storm and snow. Even the hollowness of its stem was a sign that one should empty ones heart of desire and volition.

The bamboo being used for a myriad purposes, it denotes usefulness, purposefulness, activity, economy of action, a quick mind, and resourcefulness. Its being used both for paper and brush, the bamboo is associated with writing, literature and learning. It therefore signifies both the student and the teacher, and by extension, the acquiring of knowledge; study, self-improvement. In business, the sign applies to administration.

The evergreen quality refers to constancy, fidelity and long-standing friendships.

Chung tile: There will be success; the association that bamboo has with masculine attributes indicates that the success will be in a field that is usually regarded as a man's preserve.

First tile: Correspondence will be beneficial. There is indication (bamboo referring to the written word, and the East being the reader's place) that great good will come from the initiation of correspondence. In business, new contacts will prove beneficial; in affairs of the heart, letters bearing affection.

Last tile: Study, or careful writing, will be repaid. Correspondence will have the desired effect.

In the East: Application to the written word will repay handsomely. Studies will found to have greater value than first thought; a chance reading of a paragraph that will prove valuable later.

In the South: An interesting document; a certificate; a rare book. In business, an expansion of administration. A period of relaxation and reading.

In the West: Manly pursuits; a student; a young man carrying a document. Letters received. News from afar. A person known for writing; a playwright.

In the North: A legal dispute settled favourably. Litigation settled by correspondence. A contract in your favour. Disputes involving much correspondence now settled in your favour. By seeming to retreat in the face of opposition, you will gain your cause.

Also, see further reference at the heading of the section on the Bamboo tiles.

●

(ii) THE FOUR SEASONS

SPRING   (Ch'un) 春

DELIGHT – PLEASURE – WANTONNESS – ACTIVITY

Agrees with: Li (李) Plum   Chung (中) Centre (Red)

                 Pai (白) White   Tung (東) East

Proper Guardian of: 2 Bamboo, Duck

                      5 Circles, Dragon

                      2 Wan, Double-edged sword

                      9 Wan, Heaven

Commentary

When the yellow bird was heard or seen in the spring, it was a time for the unmarried daughters to leave their homes and seek their future husbands. The ancient sign for spring showed the Sun rising, a tree stretching bare branches above it. The more modern character, a stylized version of the sign, is of similar construction to the sign for the East, shown above, which represents the rising Sun shining through the trees.

The springtime is a time of youthfulness, wantonness and temerity. It is also the time of budding growth, the return of the birds, of renewed activities. Here, therefore, are some of the follies of youth, which are seen in the Plum tile, but in spring we see more of the youthful idealism, concern and industry. It is a time of discovery; a time for shaking off the dust; for making plans and preparing for the work that lies ahead. There are dangers to be faced, to be sure. The wind may chuckle and blow, but its boisterousness may blow the blossom from the branches before it has ripened, and the fruit crop will be ruined. Yet the farmers, facing the inevitable with the renewed vigour as after a long sleep, will plan accordingly, and be prepared to change.

In brief, the follies of youth, more than tempered by zeal and industriousness.

Chung tile: Immediate success; but avoid being too rash in one's actions. Direct activity towards realistic ends.

First tile: The Spring tile, indicating renewed vigour, in the quarter to which it is proper, the East, and appearing as the first tile, is a most propitious combination, giving evidence of renewed vigour and enthusiasm in tackling whatever problems arise.

Last tile: Plans which are being made for a new venture are apt to meet with the dangers of a boisterous North wind; unintentional danger may spell mishaps, but nothing that cannot be started again. Unexpected danger from over-enthusiasm.

In the East
(or with East tile):   New plans; excitement at a new prospect. In business, new openings. In romance, a new romance!

In the South: Blossoms are gently ripened by southern breezes. A deep relationship; a serious love affair. In business, long lasting prospects. Happiness.

In the West: Some difficulties and hazards with new projects; eventual success. Plans will be discussed for a far-fetched project; it is not likely to come to fruition.

In the North: Unintentional dangers, hazards. Face all difficulties
with spirit and enthusiasm, for success will event-
ually come your way.

SUMMER   (Hsia) 夏

ACTIVITY – IDLENESS

Agrees with: Lan (蘭) Orchid   Chung (中) Centre (Red)
Pai (白) White   Nan (南) South

Proper Guardian of: 5 Bamboo, Lotus
3 Circles, Phoenix
6 Circles, Peach

Commentary

The first of the great dynasties was the Hsia. It was thought to be
mythical by many scholars until this century, when oracle bones dating
from that remote period were discovered. These were the origins of the
earliest Chinese traditions, and the pictures on the oracle bones the
foundation of Chinese writing. The sign of Hsia was a bird in flight; the
forked tail suggests a swallow, and this characteristic can still be seen in
the present-day sign for summer. Swallows' eggs were held to have
miraculous powers, and it was said that the founder of the Shang
dynasty was conceived as the result of his mother eating a swallow's egg.

It may seem strange that this sign should mean activity as well as
idleness. The allusion is to the season of summer, when all a man need do
is stand and watch the crops grow. This is not true, of course. There is a
great deal of activity going on in the summer; but even now, when there
are so many people busily engaged in summer work, it is the season for
people to take their holidays. While one half of the population is engaged
in strenuous activity, the other half are lazing in the sun.

It is the sign of farmers; anyone connected with the handling of crops;
also, those who deal in popular leisure activities. In business, deals in
commodities and leisure pursuits are favourable.

Chung tile: A substantial period of prosperity, which will eventually decline.

First tile: Investments will come to fruition, but do not leave them too long. This is a period of growth, you must harvest soon. In romantic affairs, your happiness is now, but do not presume it will last for ever without making your effort. In matters of health; good health is to be seen for a season.

Last tile: The period of prosperity is drawing to a close; look carefully to the future and whether you are not taking too nonchalant an attitude.

In the East: A time of pleasant idleness approaches. Enjoy the pleasures offered, but remember to return to important matters when the time comes.

In the South: Summer sun and South winds! A time of prosperity, success and the unexpected rewards of fortune. Unforseen gifts; a windfall; a prize. Wealth. A lucky accident. A chance encounter which will aid you in your business.

In the West: Indolence and laziness are shown by the Summer tile being in the West, where its more unfortunate characteristics show themselves in opposition to the reader. Procrastination; lassitude.

In the North: Fortune may be with you now, but it will be swept away, like standing corn before summer storms. Be prepared for unfortunate circumstances not of your own making: in business, the risks of fire, flood. In romance, a break-up; in health, an accident or an illness.

AUTUMN

(Ch'iu)

APTNESS – CONSOLIDATION – DEVOTION – MATURITY

Agrees with: Chü (菊)   Chung (中) Centre (Red)
                     Chrysanthemum   Hsi (西) West
                     Pai (白) White

Proper Guardian of: 8 Bamboo, Mushroom
                       8 Circles, Tiger
                       4 Wan, Lute
                       5 Wan, House, Stone

Commentary

A devoted but elderly wife of an emperor, knowing that he favoured a young concubine, asked him sadly whether she still had a place in his affections. 'What do you think of me, now I am old?' she wondered. He smiled and told her, 'Like a chrysanthemum in autumn.' He was not thinking of its gaudiness, but of its symbolizing nobility, of friendship and of the empress's value to him; 'in autumn' showed its aptness for its season; all the aspects of the chrysanthemum were right in their season; the empress was in her rightful place; nothing could usurp her esteem in the emperor's heart.

Autumn is a time of harvest; it is a time when food is abundant; therefore autumn signifies plenty, a time of riches. But only, however, in their season. Winter nights draw in. It is a time for consolidation.

The Chinese character for autumn (秋) combines the two signs growing grain (禾) and fire (火), indicating the season when the stubble in the corn fields is burnt to revitalize the ground for the coming year. It therefore symbolizes the time of bonfires; the burning of rubbish; getting rid of dead wood; paring down the unwanted. It is a time for reappraisal; there are hard times coming, get rid of all that is cumbersome, and replenish with fresh stock. Rid yourself of shallow acquaintances who are not friends; avoid ostentation and waste.

In business, it is a time for reappraisal; certainly not a time for embarking on new ventures. Consolidate your position, examine where economies ought to be made; cut losses. In romantic affairs, it means that you have to decide where your loyalties lie; true and trusted friends

who will stand by you in adversity are more important that idle
flatterers. In health, there is an indication that you should review your
way of life, and take care against the dangers of excess.

Chung tile: It would be rash to begin a new venture. Review your
present position, cut away hindrances and be
satisfied that everything is altogether as it should be
at the moment.

First tile: A period of prosperity and gentle enjoyment. Your
present venture is succeeding and will reward you.
Do what you can to make your present environment
more suited to your needs, rather than look
elsewhere. This is a time for stability, not change.

Last tile: Wind up those aspects of your life which are not
satisfactory. Dispose of encumbrances. Do not put
good money after bad. Concentrate on those things
which are doing well.

In the East: Maturity and devotion are the aspects which
present themselves in the reader's place. Be thankful
for long and trusted friends. Enjoy the good things
around you: see what is good and cultivate it; avoid
that which causes pain or trouble.

In the South: The gentle South winds fanning the ripened crops; a
pleasant retirement; a welcome respite; a time to sit
back and relax after an arduous and difficult period.

In the West: Dangers of wastefulness. Be careful to conserve what
you have; act wisely; use your common sense with
regards to a problem; use the wisdom of experience
in making your decision. Do not close your eyes to
reality.

In the North: To face problems which you know are inevitable, do
what you can with present resources. Do not be pro-
fligate. To the businessman: sell if you have to. To
the lover: make your choice quickly!

WINTER

(Tung)

ACCUMULATION — HOARDING — COMPLETING — LAST

Agrees with: Chu (竹) Bamboo   Chung (中) Centre (Red)
                      Pai (白) White   Pei (北) North

Proper Guardian of: 7 Bamboo, Tortoise
                      2 Circles, Pine
                      8 Wan, Knot

Commentary

More than any of the Guardian tiles Winter agrees with Pai, White, for in winter the ground is covered with snow, which has ever been a symbol of purity. The modern Chinese character for winter is such an altered form of the original that from it we can learn nothing of the symbolism. The old form was (螽), which combined (冫), ice, with (冊), meaning a fixed end. The symbolism is that of a bobbin of silk which has been unwound and spent so that there is only a last twist of thread left; underneath is water frozen hard: the year run to the end, to the days when stocks are exhausted and water is as hard as stone. For the new year, a new bobbin will have to be taken up, so the meaning is the end of one story and the beginning of another. In short; finality, the end of an episode, the last chapters of a venture.

The winter is also a time of hibernation, of living off resources. It may be a period of waiting until news of a new venture comes through. It represents a temporary period of stagnation, a time of depression, in both senses of the term. It is probably best to shut one's eyes to the difficult side of things, like the toad and the tortoise, and wait for better times to come. The occupations which went with the corresponding Noble tiles showed a fisherman in spring, a woodcarver in summer, a farmer in autumn, but in winter, a scholar. Instead of there being work and activity, it is a time for study and making plans. The present time may seem to be stagnating and getting nowhere, but it gives one the opportunity to review resources, see how best they can be used, and make plans for a time when the resources become available again. Now is the time to get out all the old schemes that were put on one side because there was no time to attend to them.

The whiteness of winter snow indicates purity. This can refer to purity of spirit in its usually accepted sense — it can also be extended to mean that which is simple and uncomplicated. The ice and snow sealing the earth have a protective quality; they do not consume nor destroy, like the fire which can be harnessed for good, yet which may escape and wreak havoc. Matters are put at one side for the time being, to give time for respite and a reappraisal when the mind is fresh. Leaving things alone for the time being, letting matters wait a while, will give one the opportunity to view things in perspective later.

The winter sign is consequently not a good sign for inaugurating new ventures, but an extremely good one for matters which require reviewing. In money matters, long term investments and savings, safe, if somewhat conservative, holdings would be better than risky but highly-paying investments, which might fall quickly. For the romantically minded, this may not be a good time for seeking a partner; indeed, you look as if you may be on your own for a while. The situation needs to be faced cheerfully, and with realism. No change is foreseen in the condition of those who inquire regarding their health.

Winter is a good sign for those whose business is in any way connected with saving or preserving; or for those who study remote and abstruse subjects.

Chung tile: This is not the time to take on new ventures. It is wisest to preserve much of your present schemes; alteration now may be for the worse. Not all change is for the better.

First tile: Not all planning need be new. There are ideas which have been put forward and forgotten. This is the time for looking again at old plans and seeing what the difficulties were, and asking whether they were so impractical after all. Perhaps if the old plans had been put into action at the time, you would not be facing your problem today.

Last tile: There is a certain finality about a tile whose interpretation is *Last* being turned up as the tile in the last place. The interpretation will pertain to the question, and the association of the tiles round it. It would indicate a finality, an end, or stop; the interpretation may be good or bad; the presence of a

green tile would mean the cessation of bad influences, for example.

In the East: In the East, the first of the Cardinal points, there is
the assurance that the end of one bobbin of silk
means that another can be picked up. Here is the
end of one chapter; the next chapter will begin soon.

In the South: The warmth of the South dispels the ice and snow.
The indications are the end of hazards and difficulties.

In the West: Winter is at its furthest from the reader; a time of
scarcity looms overhead; it may seem far away but it
would be advantageous to guard against eventual
loss.

In the North: The cold North winds blow harshly in winter. You
may have to draw on your resources; be wise, put
caution first.

——————————— • ———————————

(iii) THE THREE EXTREMES

BEGINNING (Sometimes known as **GREEN**)   (Fa) 發

INAUGURATION – BEGINNING – MANIFESTATION

Guardians: Plum
Orchid
Chrysanthemum
Bamboo

With Guardian: An Arrow

Secondary meaning: An arrow has been shot from a bow; a new venture
has already been inaugurated which will prove to be
successful.

Commentary

This tile is commonly called Green Dragon by non-Chinese speaking players. The character (發) has nothing to do with dragons, green or any other colour. The name Green has been given to it purely for the reason that it is commonly engraved on the tile in green ink — an apt colour, as green is conventionally the colour for 'all clear' or 'go ahead'. This is a happy coincidence, and will help those readers who do not know the Chinese language to remember the real meaning of the character, which is 'starting' — exactly the same as the traffic light: go ahead; beginning; start; departing. The sign shows firstly two hands, fingers apart, as if they are separating something. Beneath is a bow and a man holding an arrow; the separated hands show that the arrow has left the bow, indicating departure; a new venture; the start of something.

Fa also has in certain senses the meaning of separation, shown by the arrow leaving the bow and by the hands parting something. There is in this sign much movement, and is the Yang principle, of which Chung, the target, is the Yin.

Fa is green, the first of the five colours, the other four being sky blue, sea blue, dark green and black. Green is the colour of nature and growing things. The movement inherent in this character, and the colours of nature, indicate journeys by land or sea, depending on the associated character.

Green is also the colour of raw silk, which in many characters is taken to mean in a thread form, wound on to a bobbin. The symbolism of silk, and an arrow, therefore means the unrolling of a new project.

Green is a colour which will harmonize with many red and black tiles, producing perfect harmony. The strong amount of green in the sign combining with red and black in a sign of dubious portent will more than compensate for the negative effects of the Peach (6 Circles), Insect (7 Circles) or any Wan tiles.

It is of particularly good portent to anyone working with the land, or associated with development, or for travel. In matters of business, Fa always indicates progress and new ventures. For travellers, the outcome will be successful. For those interested in the affairs of the heart, an arrow has been set fly: in your heart or another's? The position of Fa will indicate whether it is your heart (East) or a lover's (West). In the North or South, it will only mean a love affair for a friend, although it could mean a new love for someone with whom you hoped to be romantically associated. Strictly speaking, Fa in the North or South in an indication of travel. For questions regarding health, there is a sign of recovery, though if associated with 2 Wan (Double-Edged Sword), or certain other tiles it may indicate surgery, followed by recovery. The activity and motion of Fa may indicate journeys or action towards you, rather than your taking a journey, if Fa is placed in the West.

The three Imperial Honours tiles, Fa, Chung and Pai, all indicate powerful forces working in one way or another, which can operate for your benefit if they are harnessed. The secret is in recognizing them: the oracle should tell you where they will be; in what quarter to seek assistance; in which direction lies your best course of action. The Honours tiles should always be regarded, therefore, as positive and beneficial; resources waiting to be tapped.

Chung tile:	An arrow is released; a skein of green silk is unwound; new ventures and activities are approved. There will be success in activity.
First tile: *'A Blessing'**	Definitely, the portent of a Beginning tile being turned in the first place indicates great success for new ventures. Proceed with confidence.
Last tile:	Fa as the last tile indicates that as soon as your present project is finished, another one is in hand ready to be commenced. For those in business, a particularly fortunate last tile.
In the East:	Fa shows great success in the commencing of new ventures. It also indicates travel shortly, the commencement of a journey. There is the prospect of a fresh proposal which will be approved.
In the South:	The emperor, looking South, fires an arrow. A proposition from an important person will lead to success; the associated tiles will indicate the nature.
In the West:	Proposals will be made; someone is visiting you; an arrow is pointing towards you with an indication of something beneficial; with a bamboo tile, good news; with a circle tile, tangible offering.

*See the section on the Five Cardinal Points, p. 70.

In the North: A journey by land, unless with a water tile, in which case over water to a foreign country. New ventures in the offing when the present schemes are completed.

Associations of Particular Interest
Fa-Chung-Pai   Eternity
Beginning-1 Wan   Initiation
Beginning-9 Wan   Completion

Fa-Chung-Pai ETERNITY   (Yung) 永

ETERNITY — GREAT STRENGTH — MASTERY — TOTAL DEDICATION

Commentary
The coming together of three great signs signifies great strength and power; a conjoining of great forces. There is a time of momentous decision; an event of great importance when you have to wait upon the deliberations of three important people. Such portents are significant. If you are waiting for the result of a tribunal, it will be soon. Here is a sign for correct action, and due humility and reverence, for with respectful supplication, the three emperors will not fail to listen sympathetically. In brief, an important decision will be taken shortly, over which you have little control other than to present your case as carefully as possible.

In the East: The indication is of a legal matter so close to you that you may be called to give evidence. Do so with confidence, and you will have nothing to fear. An important decision in your favour will be made shortly. Great strength of character and will.

In the South: The decision which has to be made will be tempered by humour and kindness. Mastery over circumstances.

In the West: A hearing in your absence; it is necessary for the balances, which with the Three Imperial Honours in the opposing pan of the scale are weighed heavily against you, to be balanced by good portents in the

East, or personal quarter. The sign also means
dedication to a cause, which is where you will find
help.

In the North: The best aspects of Fa-Chung-Pai are shown when
there is a linking tile in another quarter. If any one of
the three Imperial Honours is duplicated in another
quarter, the interpretation of that quarter will be
greatly assisted by the final recognition by the
highest authority. A meeting with the highest
authority.

Beginning-1 Wan   INITIATION   (Yin) 引

INITIATION — INTRODUCTION

Commentary
There is here an extremely powerful force about to create. The sign for
beginning, a man with an arrow poised to shoot, is coupled with the sign
for unity. It can be interpreted as gaining a first prize; it is an extremely
fruitful sign, and in its meaning of Initiation indicates that an honour is
going to be bestowed; in its weakest sense it may mean membership of
some society will be offered. A venture will be a success; if the query does
not specifically relate to a new venture, it will be interpreted as a forth-
coming invitation, which, being intended as an honour, it would be
churlish to refuse.

In the East: Success; a gain; an honour; an invitation. More
specifically it relates to some effort on the sitter's part
being very successful.

In the South: A successful venture; a visit to an important person;
a visit to a place which will bring surprising results.

In the West: Recognition of your efforts will bring you a letter
with gratifying news which you did not expect.

In the North: Even weakened by antipathetic forces, there is
grudging acknowledgement of your success. Praise

from an unexpected quarter. Someone whom you thought was not favourably inclined to you speaks well of your actions. A rival admits defeat. Your arrow hits the target, and enemies are silenced.

Beginning-9 Wan COMPLETION   (Ch'eng) 成

COMPLETION — FINALITY — WINDING-UP

Commentary

Fa, Beginning, is associated with the Last tile of all the suits, 9 Wan, or Heaven. It is the Beginning and the End, Alpha and Omega. It cannot be interpreted as being either a good sign or a bad one; here we have First and Last, of which the Last is Heaven. It signifies that all things have a beginning and an end; that is Fate. It is a sign which asks one to pause and ponder; it is a time for looking at less earthly things of the flesh. In answer to a question, the interpretation must here be taken to mean: is the question important enough? Are you not concerned too much with trifles? What has a beginning, must have an end, but here we have beginning and end together. Fa, the arrow being shot into the air, is full of movement and life; in T'ien we have eternal existence without change; Fa is Yang, and T'ien is Yin; the two are bound together, the two poles of a magnet are fused.

Whether Fa-T'ien appears in the East or any other quarter is im-material: wherever this association appears is a statement — not a warning, or a pronouncement, a mere acknowledgement — that what-ever happens in one's life is not going to alter the course of the Sun through the heavens.

It is time to put away worry and care, to forget ambition for a moment, and consider the quiet happiness that lies in tranquility, in the satis-faction of the completeness and order of things.

——————————————————— ● ———————————————————

CENTRE (Sometimes known as RED)   (Chung) 中

CENTRE – TARGET – TO CATCH – RECEIVING

Guardians: Spring
                      Summer
                      Autumn
                      Winter

With Guardian: Gold

Secondary meaning: A marker has been placed where a hoard has been buried; gold will be the reward of a successful discovery.

Commentary

Chung is known as the Red tile by those unfamiliar with the Chinese character (發) on account of its being engraved in red. It means Centre, the sign itself representing a target which an arrow has hit straight on. It is therefore the counterpart to Fa (Beginning), the Green tile, which shows the firing of the arrow. Fa shoots the arrow; in Chung it lands on target. Chung also means 'to catch', as if a cloth has been spread to catch fruit falling from a tree and they land in the centre. Fa represents movement; Chung the receiver of movement. Fa is the Yang principle: male, active, moving, while Chung is Yin: female, passive and still. The meaning of Chung is the fruition of efforts; the receiving of rewards; the attainment of ends. Chung therefore indicates not so much that activities are under way, but that their final scenes are about to be played. Seemingly pointless strivings are now going to be rewarded. In a sense, it also means that benefits will come from staying put, or that one's first thought ought to be nearer home. Those who are looking further afield for success and recognition would do well to take stock of what is around them; the very thing they are seeking may be under their very noses without them knowing it.

Cinnabar, Tan (丹) is the red ore of mercury, highly prized because it was believed by the old alchemists to be one of the ingredients of gold. Since cinnabar deposits indicated wealth, the brilliant red colour came mean great happiness and wealth. Indeed, another Chinese character for red (紅) is synonymous with 'lucky' or 'pleasant'. The following curious folk tale uses the symbolism of cinnabar, a tortoise, which represents the universe, and the number ten thousand, which means limitless.

'A certain holy man lived on a diet of cinnabar, and consumed it until his whole body turned red. He sat on the top of a holy tortoise, and wore no fur clothing, winter or summer. The tortoise, which shrank from the light of the Sun and the Moon, came out of its shell only once every two thousand years.'

Chung stands in a curious relationship to Fa and Pai. Whilst it is their counterpart, it is also the Central Cardinal Point tile; it has already been mentioned that the Chinese considered there to be five Cardinal Points. It is therefore important to note the connotations of self, present-time, and environment which pertain to Chung. Its appearance denotes right-mindedness, and appropriateness. It indicates smooth running, the ideal solution to problems, and satisfaction with events.

Chung tile: '*A Blessing*'	The target is in the centre; a marker shows the exact spot where a hoard of gold is hidden. Personal success will not be in doubt.
First tile:	The Chung tile in the first place indicates first consideration being given to oneself, or one's environment. It means the questioner will be acting with power and authority.
Last tile:	Chung in the last place means a return to oneself; whatever has been given out will come back; it indicates the rewards of careful investment; the reaping of the grain one has sown; eventual discovery; success after trials.
In the East:	Chung in the East denotes great concern with personal affairs, and great activity at home. Present matters are very pressing, and override considerations of long-term plans.
In the South:	The Emperor of the Middle Kingdom is in the South; the questioner will be very concerned about making improvements. It is a time to make things better; plans can be made for improving ones place;

the present is looking forward with optimism. There will be improvement.

In the West: This indicates that the questioner is setting his sights at a distant object; one is being ambitious, one may be contemplating travelling a great distance, or aspiring very loftily. Whether such aspirations are justified will depend on the associated tiles; if unsympathetic, what is being sought may be nearer at hand.

In the North: Success after tribulations. The target is eventually reached, but only after long effort.

Associations of Particular Interest

Chung-Fa-Pai	(See *Beginning*)
Centre-4 Bamboo-8 Circles	Valour
Centre-2 Circles	Peace
Centre-4 Circles	Esteem

Centre-4 Bamboo-8 Circles VALOUR   (Yung) 勇

BRAVERY — VICTORY — CONQUEST — PHYSICAL STRENGTH

Commentary

There are several possible perfect combinations of three pure tiles, but this is the most important. It combines three Yin forces to make a very powerful yang force: Tiger, Carp and Chung. The strength of the Tiger (considered a yin force in Chinese philosophy) the quarrelsome aspect of the Carp and the solidness of Chung present a formidable attacking force. Here is a decidedly belligerent group, victorious over their enemies. It means eventual triumph, either through actual physical action, or in some other attacking way. It means success will be achieved through concerted attack.

In the East: You will have the strength, determination, evidence or whatever it is that you are seeking to achieve success. You will win by force.

In the South: Concerted attack. Unexpected allies will rally to your cause.

In the West: Help will come from afar. A stranger will present the evidence you need. Success through combined efforts from both sides.

In the North: A fierce struggle is ahead. You must not give up for you will eventually have the victory.

Centre-2 Circles PEACE   (An) 安

CONTEMPLATION — SAGACITY — TRANQUILITY

Commentary

The sage contemplates in the great forest alone. It would be difficult to find two more diametrically opposite interpretations than those of the associations which Chung makes with Carp and Tiger and the one formed with Pine. While the former symbolizes active belligerence, the latter denotes passive resistance, as it has now come to be called. The meaning is that one will achieve success by taking thought, rather than through precipituous action. By withdrawing from the problem, one can review the whole picture, instead of being tied up with one aspect of it; by seeing things in perspective, a solution to the entire matter will be uncovered. Wisdom through experience is to be admired. Look carefully into the results of the action you are contemplating; immediate results may not prove to be the best solution.

In the East: Your problem will be best solved by not taking the rash action you contemplate, but by considering carefully alternative possibilities.

In the South: The matter which conerns you will be solved in an unexpected manner if for the time being you disregard it.

In the West: The matters which are troubling you are best left alone. Retire from too much activity; it is necessary now to go away for a while and contemplate.

In the North: The pine tree faces up to the storms of winter, and provides shelter for the sage there. Without the protection of furs, he is nevertheless unaffected by the snows, and does not move from the back of the holy tortoise. Disappointing news and even hardship will not trouble you in the long run; the severest storms will be weathered.

Centre-4 Circles ESTEEM   (Ch'üan) 權

RESOLUTENESS — RESPECT — AUTHORITY — HOMAGE

Commentary

Jade belongs to the Emperor, and is offered to Heaven as a token of sacrifice. Here, jade is associated with Chung, meaning both Centre and Gold. It is a perfect combination, red being the colour of living matter, green of plants, and black of the earth. Here are all the material values; but the esteem in which one is held is for one's material possessions then for attributes of character. It indicates that respect is due to the results of your actions, but these may have been made on your own behalf. The esteem denotes respect due to authority or position, not the respect which comes from an admiration of personal values. In extension, it can mean self-satisfaction.

In the East: Personal satisfaction from authority; promotion; acquisition; status.

In the South: Increased status. An offer of promotion. A business opportunity; success through negotiations. Material benefits. An honour bestowed.

In the West: Grudging respect. Homage from inferior strangers; promotion to a post abroad. Vassal states send tribute; the Emperor receves the tribute and distributes gifts to his loyal subjects.

In the North: Status brings authority but not personal loyalty. Beware those that defer to you, but who are jealous of your position. There may be resentment if you do not act in the way that you are expected to.

WHITE (Pai)

PURITY — ALONE — ABSENCE — TRUTH — LOSS

Guardians: The White tile takes on the aspect of any Guardian it replaces, and has no secondary meaning.

Commentary

White, in Chinese (白) Pai, is not really white at all, but blank, or invisible. Sometimes the tile is represented as a blank tile, which in sets made for the European market are engraved with the word 'White', and very often appears as a tile on which is engraved an empty frame. It is really therefore meant to convey either that which is not there, or that which is only apparent through the spirit, and not through physical manifestation. In Chinese mythology, anything that is described as white is usually meant to represent the supernatural; so there is the white fox, the white snake, the white tiger. It is recorded that the Prince of Kuang-Chuan attempted to excavate a grave, and in doing so frightened away a white fox. In attempting to catch the fox, he merely succeeded in injuring one of its paws. That night the Prince had a dream in which an old man, with a long white beard, came to him to ask him why he had injured his foot. When the Prince woke the next morning, his own foot was swollen and never healed till the day he died. It will be seen that here the white fox was a reincarnation, or possibly lycanthropic form, of the buried man. Other stories tell of spirits who take human form, and even marry (as in the case of the Chrysanthemum spirit), but will sometimes revert to the shape of some beast, real or mythical, but usually white. The existence of albinos in the animal kingdom caused such creatures to be regarded with especial awe because of this connection with the spirit realms, no doubt accounting for the sacredness of the Thai White Elephants.

The White tile is unusual in that it is the only tile to have no Guardian; being an absolutely blank tile it takes on the form of the Guardian it replaces, which then reveals its own symbolism. With other tiles it can form associations, whatever the colour, and inflect the interpretation accordingly. In such cases the White tile will affect the adjoining tiles, being devoid of meaning itself. It has the effect of absorbing or weakening the influences of certain associations, but much depends on the context. It does not complete the triad of colour tiles as one would expect; the so-called Green tile represents beginning, the Red tile the middle, but the White tile does not tell us that it is the end. It is blank, like a page on which nothing has been written, as if to indicate that the future is not immutable, but that the events which are to happen are partly due to fate, partly due to our making, but not irreversible. This is far removed from the Greek concept, that one cannot escape one's destiny. However, to consult an oracle and find that the future is held to be a blank page is defeating the purpose of consulting the oracle in the first place, and the matter of the blank page must be taken as a philosophical point. The blankness of the White tile gives it the symbolism of absence, so that by extension it might mean loneliness or loss. But while it refers to loss, it must be remembered that the White tile is essentially a sign of continuation, and thus, that loss is not irreparable.

In questions of speculation the White tile may be taken to mean loss; and the same token applies to questions of a romantic nature. Loss is especially indicated in the North, but if White is turned up as the last tile, its being classified as one of the Three Blessings indicates that the loss is merely a change — and as a blessing it must mean a change for the better.

On the other hand, the White tile also symbolizes purity, and by extension truth, fidelity, loyalty and spiritual happiness. It denotes simplicity of nature, candidness, naive frankness.

The seemingly opposing meanings of the White tile are of course due to its mystical nature; an interpretation is only possible through the medium of its associating tiles, its cardinal position and the substance of the question.

Chung tile:	If there is sacrifice, and the proper ways are observed, there will be success. 'New feathers and new down begin to come, white in colour. The administration of a truthful regime imperceptibly bears the weight of a new body.'
First tile:	A period of absence, or loneliness. Success will come about through making personal sacrifice.
Last tile: 'A Blessing'	There will be loss, which will bring change. Success will be brought about firstly through loss.
In the East:	Success is indicated through truthfulness, sobriety and uprightness. It may be necessary to make certain

personal sacrifices in order to attain something which is more worth-while.

In the South: A journey on one's own is indicated. It will be of a serious, but not a sad nature.

In the West: Absence of a loved one. Friends or loved ones will be called away, leaving you without help. In business, important associates will be away unavoidably. In love, a parting.

In the North: Loss, but if the White tile is the last turned, loss turning to change. Here is the end of one cycle and the beginning of another. It can also mean the revelation of news which has long been hidden from you. A mystery at long last discovered; the truth finally unveiled.

Associations of Particular Interest

Pai-Fa-Chung   See Fa
White-8 Circles   White Tiger
White-9 Circles   Nobility

White-8 Circles   WHITE TIGER   (Pai Hu) 白虎
(in its realm)

PROTECTION — HIDDEN STRENGTH — SUPPORT IN NEED

Commentary

The White Tiger is one of the astrological palaces, and refers to the third quarter of the sky, representing the West. The appearance of White and Tiger in the West sector is extremely auspicious, and a sign of good fortune. This is an unusual association, formed of a pure black and a pure white tile. Having at one and the same time no colour and yet all colours, this represents the unity of Yin and Yang in one — so self involved that there is nothing outside it. Two are totally enwrapped as one, excluding all else. To geomancers the White Tiger represented the

Yin lines of force which they believed traversed the earth. As such, the Yin lines of the White Tiger were the counterpart to the Yang lines of the Azure Dragon.

White is the colour of the supernatural; here we have an indication of supernatural or unexpected, if not unexplained, assistance. It may signify inner fortitude in times of trouble, help from an unknown source, a new ally. As with all associations, the meaning of white becomes merged into that of the association. White Tiger negates the aspect of loss that is inherent in white, and any negative aspects inherent in the Black tile.

In the East: Unexpected help from an ally; in time of danger or trouble there will be generous help from an unforeseen source.

In the South: Plans and ideas meet with approval. A powerful organization wishes to assist.

In the West: A distant friend comes to aid unexpectedly. Good Fortune.

In the North: Plans which had to be dropped will suddenly become of interest to other people. Success after initial failure.

White-9 Circles NOBILITY   (Kuan) 官

ENNOBLEMENT — INVITATION — RECOGNITION

Commentary
The Unicorn, 9 Circles, is a perfect tile, and as it bears all three colours it is not adversely affected by the White tile. Its purity is enhanced. In combination with the White tile it takes on the new meaning of Nobility, whose lesser meaning is an invitation by a person of high rank. This interpretation would therefore indicate success in one's particular field, and that this success has evidently been recognized by someone in authority. It is a satisfactory combination, therefore, which indicates that one's past actions have been just and proper, in order that one's deeds should be so recognized, or that the course of action one is

contemplating must, if properly carried through, meet with eventual success and recognition.

In the East: The course of action which is being planned will be successful, and lead to a recognition by other people.

In the South: There will be success in those fields which have to do with service to the public, and your actions will not go unnoticed.

In the West: Your activities in many fields have been discussed and you have attracted the attention of someone important, who is as yet unknown to you.

In the North: The difficulties under which you are at present labouring will shortly be removed, and you will receive commendation for your working under extreme difficulty.

———————— • ————————

(iv) THE FOUR DIRECTIONS

EAST (Tung) 東

SELF — MASTERY — HOME

Guardians: Plum
Spring

With Guardian: Dawn

Secondary Meaning: Yellow is the colour of the earth, from which all things emanate. An abundance of treasure which might pass unrecognized, until the morning light illumines it.

Commentary
The word Tung (東) has two distinct, but inextricably linked,

meanings: East and Master. Readers who are familiar with the game of Mah Jongg will know that it is the East player who deals, who has mastery over his round of the game. It is not a conventional notion; East and master are two English translations of differing aspects of the same word. It follows that the sense of East must also have the sense of mastery. If East appears in the East sector, it means that the questioner is master; its appearance in other sectors, or with other tiles, will sometimes indicate mastery over a craft, over a problem, or being in charge of a situation. Conversely, for East to appear in a less favourable position may indicate subjection to the mastery of some other person or circumstance.

On the whole, however, East very often represents the questioner, and its appearance in particular associations may represent the questioner in different situations.

Since the East sector generally represents home territory, East may also refer to the questioner's home or family, especially if the question posed touches upon the subject of the family, home or house.

The interpretation of East through its written character when the tile is in a favourable position shows a new day beginning; the dawn of a new life; a new project; a fresh start. It signifies hope, confidence and ambition; enthusiasm and optimism. It indicates the renewed vitality and spirit of co-operation that comes from a change of leadership.

The qualities shown by East are principally leadership. Where East is in a position which obviously refers to the questioner, such as the Chung tile, or in the East tiles themselves, it will indicate qualities of leadership in the questioner himself. In other positions, the reference to leadership moves progressively away from the subject, so that in the West it may actually indicate subjection to authority; the notion of leadership is transferred from the subject to those in opposition. If East appears in more than one sector, it is generally understood to refer to the continuation of a project. Overall, its secondary meaning is one of optimism, so that even at its most unfavourable positions it continues to radiate confidence.

Generally an excellent sign for those engaged in new projects. For those about to marry, a most auspicious beginning. In questions regarding the family, a sign of a new baby.

Tung-Hsi (東西)

The tiles Tung and Hsi together form the Chinese word Tunghsi, or *things*. It is an exceptional combination, and is immediately read in its literal sense as meaning objects, things, materials, and so on.

Chung tile: The Sun rises above the trees; a new day. Increase. There will be success in a new venture. An auspicious beginning for a new project.

First tile: East in the first tile place indicates master. It shows that the questioner is master of the situation. The questioner will control the outcome, and make the pertinent decisions on which the success of the project depends.

Last tile: That which was begun must be finished. There is a reminder of one's obligations. In the end is the beginning. No job can be counted a success until it is finished. Attend to things which are yet outstanding, and a fresh project can be started with renewed confidence.

In the East: The East tile in the East quadrant is most auspicious; it indicates that things have begun well, and will continue to do so, under the direction of the questioner.

In the South: There is less emphasis on the questioner and more on schemes and plans. There is indication of successful schemes and plans being accepted. Journeys undertaken will be very advantageous.

In the West: East here represents the authority to which the questioner is subject; generally it means that the questioner is highly regarded by those who are above him. Satisfactory acceptance of the offerings.

In the North: In the depth of winter, the dawn is always welcomed. The few warming rays of sunlight are eagerly awaited. Situations which have proved difficult will be smoothed over. Even the worst of problems can be solved. East here is the silver lining behind the darkest cloud.

East-5 Circles   BENEVOLENCE   (Jên) 仁
(Dragon in its realm)

MAGNANIMITY — UNSELFISHNESS — KINDNESS — MERCY

Commentary

The association of 5 Circles (Dragon) with East is known as the Dragon in its Realm, one of four such associations. It has already been pointed out that the associations of the Four Fabulous Beasts in their Realms are always considered to be perfect, it being understood that the black of the Realm tile is changed to the spiritual white. The dragon is not the monster of Western mythology, but rather, a benevolent spirit, and is the symbol of imperial majesty. In its realm, the dragon is stable and tranquil; the Emperor is not concerned with wars and struggles, and can afford to be gracious. Those who fear the Emperor's wrath for their misdoings can approach without trepidation, for he is disposed to be merciful.

In the East: The Dragon is in its Realm in association with the East tile, but also by virtue of being in the East quadrant. This is particularly auspicious, as it puts the reader in the position of being able to be merciful. You will have the opportunity to gain respect by your delicate handling of a problem which is brought to you by a person in distress.

In the South: This association indicates that the benevolent power is near at hand. Work which must undergo thorough criticism will be acceptable.

In the West: The position of the Dragon opposite the questioner indicates that the authority to whom the questioner is subject will regard proposals benignly.

In the North: Concerns or dealings abroad or at a distance are especially favoured; an independent assessment by someone whose authority does not extend to the questioner will be favourable.

———————————   ●   ———————————

SOUTH   (Nan)

GROWTH — PROGRESS — DEVELOPMENT

Guardians: Orchid
                    Summer

Secondary meaning: The Sun, who lives in the South, brings an
                     abundance of vegetation. There the earth is
                     abundant, and men can resort to contemplation
                     while the harvest ripens.

Commentary

Plants turn towards the Sun, and that being in the South, plants turn to
the South. The lodestone, which was used by early mariners, will turn to
lie along a South-North line; the Chinese (with no less logicality than
the Europeans who took it to be pointing North) assumed that it must be
pointing South, too. All Nature turns to the South. The Emperor, in
whom dwells the soul of his people, also faced the South. In order that
the Emperor may always look towards the South, not only the Imperial
Palace, but all the City, and indeed all cities, were built in a regular
alignment, North to South. The gates to the city were in the South, so
that as a subject approached his Emperor he would be continually facing
the North. Houses were therefore built with their doors facing North, so
that citizens would always face the Emperor. It eventually became so
enmeshed in the language that to face North or South meant to face
towards or away from the door. By further extension, to face southwards
indicated superiority. The superior person would face South, illumined
by the Sun, and his inferiors would stand to the South of him. To travel
southwards therefore indicates one is superior, whereas the converse is
to be sent to the cold North, indicating subjection.

The character for South, Nan (南), is generally understood to
represent the abundance of vegetation that one finds in the warmer
regions. The character shows boundaries (☐) enclosing plants which
are bursting beyond their confines, so abundantly do they grow. The
South tile therefore means abundance, but because of the sense that the
plants may overreach their boundaries, it can also mean excess.

Its basic interpretation is growth. For plans which have already begun, the indication is that such plans will continue to be fruitful. An end is not yet in sight. Less advisable are new projects, for those which are current are not yet completed. There is also the danger that present involvements may get out of hand unless they are carefully watched. Fields may be full of the plants sown by the farmer, but there are also weeds which will grow copiously without the farmer's help. In a cautionary sense, South can mean excess, not only of things which are beneficial, but those which may become a burden. Excess may mean profit or profligacy. The South tile is favourable in East or South positions. In the former it will mean abundance, merit or material gain for the questioner; in the latter it indicates fruitful journeys. It is only moderately favourable in the West quadrant where it often signifies precaution against waste or carelessness. In the North there are indications of opposition and criticism of the questioner's plans and proposals.

In matters of the heart, South indicates the continuing of a present relationship; in matters of health, South reveals continuing good health, or in the North, recovery after an illness. South and North tiles together show opposition; in the East, South and North together indicate competition that the questioner will be able to overthrow; in the South, South and North together mean excess and waste; in the West, an opponent, and in the North, loss because of waste.

Generally speaking, South indicates continuing progress, development and expansion. It is usually favourable, but cautions against needless and excessive waste. On the whole, it refers to material possessions, but in the South may indicate travel. It is the Realm of the Phoenix (3 Circles), and as such indicates prosperity.

Chung tile: Luxuriant abundance is in the centre; the Emperor is facing South and is pleased with the news a messenger brings. A fortunate encounter with a person of high rank.

First tile: A period of prosperity. There is immediate gain from your efforts; your work is highly regarded; a reward is granted.

Last tile: A reminder that there are matters still to be cleared. You are living off merit or material benefits which though fruitful are not endless. Off with the old before on with the new.

In the East: South indicates material gains and benefits; a period of affluence; successful efforts are to be rewarded. Satisfaction through continuing achievements.

In the South: A long journey, which may be for pleasure, or business. If the latter it will be successful. You will accompany a person of high rank on a journey.

In the West: An affluent period is drawing to a close. Beware of overspending. Times may appear to be fruitful, but Winter follows Autumn unfailingly. A gentle caution against rashness.

In the North: Conflict and opposition. It may be that your plans or proposals do not meet with official approval. The malign aspects are only temporary however, but be prepared for setbacks.

South-3 Circles   PROSPERITY   (Fu) 富
(Phoenix in its Realm)

ABUNDANCE — AFFLUENCE — MERIT — REWARD

Commentary

The phoenix only appears in times of happiness and prosperity, at other times returning to its own land. Its presence in its own realm therefore indicates that a stable period of happiness and prosperity is at hand. It may either signify that an ambition is shortly to be achieved, and that the satisfaction of such achievement will lead to a serenity of mind, or that external circumstances will shortly change in such a way that one's problems and worries will be taken away. It shows satisfaction with one's circumstances, whether or not this has been the achievement of ambitions, or an adjustment to a happy acceptance of an improved situation.

In the East: There is satisfaction through the achievement of one's ambitions through the success of one's endeavours. Realization of one's ambitions; efforts rewarded. Recognition. Prosperity after labour.

In the South: A period of affluence. One reaps the rewards of one's past efforts. A change of fortune for the better.

In the West: Reconciliation with opposing or competing forces; an end of squabbles; peace after frictions. Long enmities forgotten. Contentment with one's colleagues.

In the North: Obstacles will be overcome at last. Stumbling blocks which have impeded progress will be removed. Sources of irritation will disappear; quarrelsome colleagues will become more affable. Contentment and serenity.

————————————— ● —————————————

WEST   (Hsi)

OBJECTIVE — SUBJECTION — SEPARATION

Guardians: Chrysanthemum
Autumn

With Guardian: Guests

Secondary meaning: The Dowager Empress of the West appears as a mortal, although when she transforms herself she has a leopard's tail, tiger's teeth, and wears a tiara. She is attended by blue birds.

Commentary

The origin of the character for West is obscure; it is popularly supposed to represent birds settling on their nests, but a more scholarly view is that it originally represented a parcel or baggages, which is why the Chinese Tung-Hsi (East-West) means 'things'. The West is the direction 'to which all things go' — even the Sun declines in the West. The West can therefore mean finality, or closing. It can mean the end of a cycle, completion of a project, the end of a venture. It may signify a warning to avoid putting good money after bad.

In another sense, West signifies gentle happiness. The setting Sun, the time of evening, is the time when work is finished, and with friends one can spend a few pleasant hours in conversation and relaxation. The character for 'spirits' is similar to the character for 'West' because it is in the evening that one would drink a glass with friends. This 'spirits' character is also the horary sign for 5-7pm, the time when one would finish the day's work.

Whether West is taken to mean decline, or happy leisure, will depend on where it appears, and the associating tiles. If it appears in the North, or winter quarter, then the evenings will be long and cold, but if in the South, then the evenings will be spent in peaceful relaxation.

The interpretation of West is as the Objective: for it is the opposite of East. Since East represents the questioner, then West represents his goal, the ends to which he strives. Similarly, just as East represents the home, and the environment close at hand, so West means distant places. Again, whereas East represents mastery, so West represents subjection.

The qualities shown by West are devotion, loyalty, duty. It shows travel, projects at a distance, domination. If West appears in the East sector, this is favourable, for it shows the questioner having mastery over the situation. If West appears in the West sector, the signs are one of pessimism. West does not indicate favourable conditions for beginning new projects, but favourable opportunities for bringing existing schemes to a close.

In the North, it shows unfavourable influences: subjection to authority, decline of assets, the winding-up of affairs. However, if in association with Red and Green tiles, these unfavourable influences can be balanced, or converted into beneficial ones.

Chung tile:	Friends call for a glass of wine and spend the evening; figuratively, continuing enjoyment of prosperity; retirement; gentle relaxation. A sign of continuing stillness.
First tile:	West as the first tile indicates subjection; the questioner must carefully consider his relationships with those about him. He will not be in control of the situation, and will have to tread carefully.
Last tile:	Successful completion of a project. An imminent end; final closing. Loose ends are sorted out. Problems satisfactorily resolved.
In the East:	West in the East indicates harmonious relations; a

balance of subject and master. Those in authority
will be favourable.

In the South: Continuing prosperity; maturity; final growth. The
harvesting of the fruits of one's labours. Reaping the
benefits.

In the West: Subjection to authority. Decline. Unexpected.

In the North: Unfavourable views. An end of resources. Projects
brought to an end before completion. Unnecessary
journeys. Dearth of resources; lean years. The questioner subject to hostile criticism.

West-White-8 Circles   White Tiger in its Palace
For interpretation of the three tiles, West, White, and 8 Circles, see
under White-8 Circles.

——————————————— • ———————————————

NORTH   (Pei) 北

ENDURANCE — RELIABILITY — DISTANCE — OPPOSITION

Guardians: Bamboo
Winter

With Guardian: Separation. The North is the antithesis of the Sun;
its mansions are never visited by the Sun; this
indicates cold and separation.

Commentary
The harsher climates of the North indicate endurance; yet the North
Star, fixed and unchanging in its place, is the symbol of the Emperor.
The North is a symbol of stern qualities, discipline, and authority.
Confucius said: 'He who exercises government by means of his virtue
may be compared to the pole star, which keeps its place while all the
other stars move round it.'
Lines of force flow between North and South; the lodestone indicates
this, that there will be easy passage from one extreme to another, or the

continuation of projects which follow the least line of resistance. To cross barriers will be difficult, and there will be opposition to change. Since North represents the highest authority, it is well to be subject to such higher authority, and to rule one's subjects firmly and justly. There is communication from above to below, but there are difficulties encountered outside. The North indicates an attention to duty, and to see that there is no neglect; it requires an obedience to the regulations, or there will be retributions. It shows that one must supervise carefully, and see that those who are responsible to us are fulfilling their obligations.

Depending on its place, and the associated tiles, North can mean hardship and endurance, or authority. It may mean opposition, or it can mean strength — it always conveys the implication of authority, whether acting on the subject's behalf, or against him. It can also be taken to mean distance, if this is pertinent to the question. Generally speaking, North refers to a close-knit group, and the actions within that group. It may mean a family unit, or a small company, or an enclosed region. It refers to things that are closely related, but which may become separated, such as close members of a family who are separated; or branches of a company in different places; or the government of a local authority separated from a distant governing body. It warns against letting outsiders into that closely knit group; against strangers coming into the family, against other companies coming between the parent and subsidiary companies, against territorial encroachment. It can refer to long journeys, long periods of time, hard work, and endurance. It does not indicate that these will not be rewarded, however. It may show the prospect of lean times, and warn against prodigality. As a symbol of winter, it can indicate that there will be hard times ahead, and that it is as well to take precautions against future losses.

In matters of the heart, North indicates a long and enduring relationship which may have its problems, but that these will be overcome. In the South, there is a very favourable sign for a lifetime attachment. In matters of health, North indicates a chronic illness; its place in the East or South will indicate recovery. In matters of travel, North indicates long journeys; in the North, that the journeys will mean long separation.

North is a realm of the Black Tortoise, indicating long life and sagacity.

Chung tile: Authority. You will acquire authority; it must be exercised justly and firmly. Consolidation.

First tile: A difficult task is presented. Ice and snow. But under the rays of the rising Sun, they will be melted away. Strength to overcome difficulties.

Last tile: A warning. The winter is not over. It is necessary to conserve resources against difficult times in the future. The foreshadowing of conflict with authority.

In the East: Snow under the rising Sun. There are problems at present, but there will be strength from those in authority to overcome difficulties.

In the South: Distance; communication between extremes. This may indicate a long journey, or long distance communications. It indicates the merging of opposing forces, the reconciliation of Yang and Yin. It is a beneficial sign for the joining of opposing forces.

In the West: A warning of decline; progression to winter; the setting Sun and the approach of winter. It is not advantageous to embark on new ventures.

In the North: Strength in authority; opposition to authority. It is well to work with those who may oppose you, since the power lies in their hands. It is not advantageous to try and flout authority, or risk any chancy ventures.

North-7 Bamboo   MEMORY   (I) 憶
(Tortoise in its Realm)

SAGACITY − REMINISCENCE − REGRET − REMORSE

Commentary

The tortoise is one of the Heavenly Palaces of old Chinese astrology. Properly known as the Black Tortoise, the position of the tortoise next to the black North tile indicates that the tortoise has returned to its mansion. The North is the sign of winter; the tortoise hibernates through the winter, so that we read this association as memory, reminiscences of the rest of the active year. It is a sign of inaction, hibernation, preservation. Through memory we understand wisdom and sagacity; but also there is the association with memorial tablets and things past — regrets, remorse, things left undone, things which ought not to have been done.

In the East: In the East, we see the Sun rising, a sign of spring and the dawn. Regeneration after long stagnation. New ideas after hibernation. Renewal after rest.

In the South: The sign of summer — memory is put to good use, to study, to learning, and teaching. Storage of information; the writing of histories; compiling of documents.

In the West: Declining memory; reminiscences, regrets. Recollections. The writing of reports and letters after events.

In the North: Stagnation; storage; preservation. A time for inaction, and for reviewing past action.

North-9 Bamboo   STRENGTH   (Li) 力

FORTITUDE – RESISTANCE – TENACITY – PURPOSE

Commentary

By Strength is meant the ability to resist adversity, not the active extravert force that might be used for construction or destruction. It is shown by the willow in the face of the North wind, which it is able to resist: 'There are some winds that only please the willow.' It indicates firmness of purpose and steadfastness. In spite of opposition, the questioner will not weaken and will achieve his aims.

It is a warning not to give in to adversity, not to release the grip on what is rightfully held; not to stray from the right path; not to be tempted into accepting the inferior. By not giving in to temptation, by resisting that which has immediate appeal, there will be greater benefits to be gained.

In the East:	The rising Sun shows the offer of several promises; but if they are rejected, there will be even greater opportunities later. Resist the inferior offer.
In the South:	Achievement of purpose; by having waited, success will now come. Adverse conditions will soon pass. Additional strength to achieve one's purpose.
In the West:	Arguments and opposition will be overcome. There will be quarrels and disagreements, but through tact and diplomacy, the problems will be resolved.
In the North:	Fierce opposition will be overcome. Stormy times and difficulties, but with strength of purpose all will be resolved.

——————————— • ———————————

(v) THE BAMBOO TILES

 (Chu)

The high esteem in which the bamboo is held has been discussed already as the last of the Four Nobles on page 82. The T'ai-P'ing Imperial Encyclopaedia tells of the scholar Wang Hui-Chih who once lodged for a short time in an empty house, but nevertheless took the trouble to plant some bamboo. When asked why he should do this, when he would not be staying there long enough, he replied, 'How can one live without this gentleman?'.

This indicates the reverence, almost awe, in which this versatile plant was held. Being evergreen, it is appropriate that most of the Bamboo tiles should be engraved in green. They are almost all positive in their significance, and help to counteract any danger portents manifested by less favourable signs. Nearly all the Bamboo tiles are 'watery', including such symbolism as the Toad, Carp, Willow Tree and so on. Their effect is generally complacent, gentle, soothing, healing.

While the majority of the aspects of bamboo are good signs, they may not seem to be so highly regarded by the inquirer who is seeking rapid action, sudden fortune, or the success of grandiose schemes. The indications are nearly all of gentleness.

The bamboo indicates the written word, and the type of people portrayed by bamboo are therefore writers, teachers, literary people. In business, the administration side is covered, rather than the practical side. Such trades as are covered by the bamboo will be in reference to the bamboo's use in light building: hence possibly light construction work.

If the bamboo has a negative side at all, it will be perhaps in the insistence upon the letter of the law, perhaps a too niggling attitude to rules and regulations which will lead to quarrels (4 Bamboo, Carp). Or else it might indicate one who is so concerned with the theory that he forgets the practice (8 Bamboo, Mushroom), or one who tends to day-dream too much, letting things of practical use slide by (7 Bamboo, Tortoise).

On the whole, however, a Bamboo tile is a welcome sign.

1 Bamboo   PEACOCK   (K'ung) 孔

BEAUTY – DIGNITY – HIGH RANK – SELF-ESTEEM

Guardian: Plum.

With Guardian: The Bride.

Secondary meaning: The Bride is arrayed in all her finery; but she is so conscious of her own beauty that she forgets her duties to her new husband. A warning to wives to be faithful.

Commentary

The 1 Bamboo is the first of the suit tiles and is distinguished by the emblem of a bird. Being the first tile, it means the first of something; it can mean great success, by being the foremost in authority, or taking the first prize, or attainment. It is generally a sign of good fortune, indicating success. In the ancient Spirit Manuals, 1 was universally a sign of good fortune, and the only number on which all the manuals were in total agreement.

It indicates the embarking on new enterprises, the joys of setting off on journey, departure for a new life. It indicates marriage, especially if the questioner is a girl of marrying age and if the tile appears in the East. It shows success in examinations or with new projects. It is the sign of beauty, and indicates admiration, either for oneself or for one's work. It indicates care with appearance, tidiness. The professions indicated are those in which personal appearances matter. The warnings indicated by this tile are to guard against self-indulgence, vanity, disregard of others. In caring too much for oneself, one may damage the sensibilities of those around.

Chung tile: The appearance of 1 Bamboo as the Chung tile indicates personal success, attainment, and great fortune. Your wish will be granted.

First tile: The appearance of 1 Bamboo in the first place indicates the successful start of a new venture; promotion, or travel. There is joy and adventure.

Last tile: 1 Bamboo in the last place indicates a warning against being too concerned with ones own ends; it is a warning against letting success go to ones head.

In the East: 1 Bamboo in the East indicates great success in a new venture; for a girl it indicates marriage.

In the South: Peacocks vaunting themselves in the summer sun; there will be great success. Wealth and good fortune.

In the West: An indication that one is forgetting obligations to others. A warning against self-indulgence.

In the North: Sudden fortune in adversity. 1 Bamboo in the North indicates personal success in cases of adversity, but the questioner should guard against self-congratulation.

1 Bamboo, 1 Circle   VANITY   (I) 伕

The Peacock and the Pearl indicate Vanity; indulgence; luxury. It is a warning against shallowness, against letting attention falter, against fawners and flatterers, against those who are spiteful and jealous, and against prodigality. Too much concern with one's own well-being may blind the vainglorious to the plots of others. Guard against waste and extravagance.

2 Bamboo   DUCK

(Ya)

FIDELITY – DEVOTION – AFFECTION – MARRIAGE

Guardian: Spring

With Guardian: The Young Man

Secondary meaning: A young man seeking to marry. Ducks stay together for life; this indicates marital faithfulness, and long devotion.

Commentary

2 Bamboo is one of the few tiles which have a special significance in the game of Mah Jongg; if this tile is taken from another player to win the game it is known (in certain circumstances) as 'scratching a carrying pole', and the player is entitled to maximum points. This tile is therefore a particularly fortunate one for the player who is able to 'scratch' it — less fortunate for the player who has been robbed of it. It is therefore an object of good omen for the questioner.

Its significance is fidelity and devotion, and the satisfaction from having completed one's obligations dutifully and punctiliously. It indicates successful personal relationships. For those whose business calls for them to deal with other people, it indicates satisfaction and progress. For those enquiring about romantic matters, it indicates successful relationships. Of the professions, it indicates those which involve caring: nursing, medicine, social work. In matters of health, it indicates that through caring and nursing, the patient will recover from the illness.

Chung tile: 2 Bamboo is a sign of good fortune, and is associated with the Spring; success will come in the Spring and Summer months.

First tile: Prospects of a new relationship of a long-lasting and intimate nature. Marriage. For those already married, marriage of a friend or relative.

Last tile: Enduring satisfaction. Successful continuity.

In the East: A sudden happy chance; unexpected luck. Prospects
                    of new relationships.

In the South: Happiness. Contentment with loved ones. A genial
                    meeting. Friendly relationships. A wedding.

In the West: The gathering together of things. Long-term plans;
                    formulation of projects for future reference. Inaug-
                    uration of long-term projects.

In the North: Marriage of a relative. Thoughts of retirement.

2 Bamboo, 2 Wan   COMPANIONSHIP   (P'èng) 朋

The appearance of 2 Wan with 2 Bamboo indicates two friends, especially two male friends of long standing. It shows harmonious companionship and trust. It can mean partnership in business, or a joint
undertaking, depending on the nature of the question. Its indication is
mutual trust.

Other Associations

With 5 Bamboo, Lotus, the indication is of contentment and satisfaction. If two 2 Bamboo tiles appear together, it is a sign of great fortune,
and a sure indication of a marriage.

———————————— • ————————————

3 Bamboo   TOAD   (Min)

DISAPPOINTMENT — OVERAMBITION — FRUSTRATION

Guardian: Bamboo

With Guardian: The Moon

Secondary meaning: The hare lives in the Moon, where it distils the Elixir
                    of Life.

Commentary

The toad lives in the Moon (the Chinese believe that the dark patches on the surface of the Moon represent a toad, rather than the Man in the Moon) and is therefore the symbol of the unattainable. It represents dreams — day-dreams, and wishful thinking — rather than attention to reality. There is nothing wrong in dreams and plans, provided that these are realistic; if one sets one's sights too high, or one's ambitions are not realistic, then there will only be disappointment and frustration.

However, if the dreams are combined with feminine intuition, as shown by Peach (6 Circles) then dreams may be realized. Two 3 Bamboo tiles together means brightness, and hence success, but if they are in opposite quarters, then they signify eclipse and disappointment. With 3 Wan it indicates the three-legged toad — the unobtainable or unattainable. If the Toad is shown with cautious tiles, or tiles showing wealth, especially in the East or South, it can mean the accumulation of wealth through interest. In questions of the heart, the Toad does not show lasting relationships. In matters of business, it indicates caution. the professions indicated are those in which caution and attention to detail are called for.

Chung tile:	There will be disappointment; do not attempt too much; modify your demands.
First tile:	The Toad as the first tile indicates ambitious plans. It is well to modify these lest they prove to be too difficult to complete.
Last tile:	Disappointment. Plans may only be in the idea stage; they must be pruned if there is to be success.
In the East:	The Toad in the East indicates disappointment, but if combined with a feminine tile, can indicate the realization of plans through the adoption of intuitive courses of action. With Circle tiles, may indicate the accumulation of wealth.
In the South:	If there are Circle tiles associated, 3 Bamboo can mean the accumulation of wealth through banking. South tends to negate the negative aspects of this tile, which generally indicates disappointment.

| *In the West:* | You have over-ambitious plans for others. They resent your interference; your expectations are too high. |

| *In the North:* | Contemplation and meditation. Reconsider all plans carefully; do they truly represent what is realistic? |

3 Bamboo, 8 Wan DISCOVERY   (Hsien) 現

The presence of the Knot obviates the disappointing aspects of this tile, and enhances those meanings of contemplation. It indicates consideration and deliberation, and the solution to what appear to be insurmountable difficulties. Slowly but surely, the knots will be unravelled.

———————————— ● ————————————

4 Bamboo CARP   (Li)

ABUNDANCE — LONGEVITY — DETERMINATION

| *Guardian:* | Orchid |

| *With Guardian:* | The Two Lovers |

| *Secondary meaning:* | The Orchid and the Carp, the two beauteous things of nature, the inspiration for poets and painters. The sign is a good omen for lovers. |

Commentary

The Carp has a wealth of symbolic meanings, and has many different interpretations, depending on its position and its association with other tiles. It indicates both youth and longevity, and hence enduring relationships from youth to old age. If the Carp is taken as an extra tile from a tower, it indicates great success. Being the symbol of gold, it signifies wealth. Being prized for its beauty, it signifies culture and refinement. Being the subject of the meditations of sages, it signifies discernment, but it also indicates a quarrelsome nature. With tiles which indicate animal life (the Tiger, the Duck, the Tortoise), it indicates wrangles and quarrels. With tiles which indicate vegetative life (the Orchid, the Lotus, the Three Trees), it indicates scholarly refinement. With tiles of an inanimate nature (Jade, Lute, House), it signifies serenity and fulfilment of purpose. With the White tile is signifies spirituality and religious meditation, prayer, withdrawal from worldly life. It can indicate success in examinations, especially in association with 1 Wan. With regard to affairs of the heart, it indicates a youthful romance. In business, it signifies the accumulation of wealth. With regard to personal relationships in business, or the distant family, it can signify quarrels and contention. *Its realm is water; therefore it is not affected by the Cardinal points*, its significance in the different regions depends on the associating tiles only. With 6 Bamboo, Water, it signifies abundance, knowledge, wisdom, accumulation. It takes on a negative aspect only with 3 Wan, Earth, for the carp cannot live in the Earth element. Hence, with 3 Wan, it is necessary to see what the third associating tile is; if Water, it remains auspicious. Otherwise, the Earth tile signifies the end of whatever is the interpretation of the other two tiles in the triad.

Chung tile: The Carp indicates attention to detail; scholarly pursuits; success, especially in examinations. It indicates good fortune through steady efforts.

First tile: The commencement of studies; steady progress. The accumulation of wealth. For the young it indicates the beginning of a romance; for the older it shows the enjoyment of one's labours.

Last tile: Success as the result of one's endeavours. Good fortune; good health in old age; longevity.

*In the East:**   Generally, an indication of good fortune.

*In the South:**   Scholarly pursuits; literature, poetry, and music.

*In the West:**   Soldierly endurance, fortitude.

*In the North:**   Continuing health.

*But see note above, on the fact that the meaning is not altered by the Cardinal points.

4 Bamboo, Centre, 8 Circles   VALOUR   *See* **CENTRE**

4 Bamboo, 4 Wan   RECONCILIATION   (Tiao) 調

The Carp is here the symbol of painting and literature, just as the Lute is the symbol of music. The indication is therefore the enjoyment of cultural pursuits, and the end to old quarrels. It is a symbol of reconciliation, between parted lovers, between broken families, between friends who had quarrelled. It indicates the renewal of old business partnerships in a spirit of renewed understanding. It is the symbol of trust, the forgetting of injuring, the bridging of rifts. In matters of health, it indicates the healing of wounds, the successful outcome of an operation, recovery from an illness. It indicates diplomacy, tact, renewal of faith.

4 Bamboo, 7 Wan   REWARD   (Chiang) 獎

The Carp appearing here is the symbol of wealth, the reward for diligence and patience. It indicates success in examination, return of favours, gratitude, and acknowledgement. The sign of the Stars represents the Dragon Gate; when the Carp enters the Dragon Gate it too becomes a Dragon. It is changed, like the pawn reaching the opposite side of a chess board. Service and loyalty are rewarded.

———————————————   ●   ———————————————

5 Bamboo   LOTUS   (Lien) 蓮

CLARITY – VISION – CONTEMPLATION – DECISION

Guardian: Summer

With Guardian: A Child

Secondary meaning: The Child born in a lotus. Intuition and Recognition. Innocence and purity.

Commentary

The lotus is a mystic symbol, and is related to spiritual things. The beautiful flower is found growing in the swamp, among the weeds, noxious vapours, and water-beasts. It represents beauty emerging from the mire. It shows that there can be untainted innocence in the most unlikely places. It is therefore a symbol of that which cannot be corrupted: impartiality; truth; fairness; honesty; piety. It indicates the freeing of the soul through perception; the ability to see through schemes. It is a sign of inner vision, one that is able to penetrate the mask of deception, and pierce the veneer of guile. It shows the uncovering of hidden secrets; the end of deceit; a guard against fraud. Through contemplation comes truth; by taking thought one is able to pierce the schemes and stratagems of those who seek to do harm. It reveals imposters, shames dissemblers, exposes tricksters.

The lotus in the swamp can be likened to a beautiful lady in her bath. It is the symbol of spiritual paradise, and the cleansing of the soul. In questions of the heart, it symbolizes the union of souls, of pure unsullied love. In business matters, it shows the exposure of deceitful methods.

Chung tile: The Lotus shows the attainment of ends when their value is appreciated. You will not get what you are seeking now, but you will find something better in its place.

First tile: The Lotus shows the attainment of happiness through spiritual satisfaction; a realization of the worthlessness of material possessions and a higher regard for immaterial values.

Last tile: Although the situation may not seem to be what is immediately wanted, out of the morass will emerge something of greater value than could have been anticipated.

In the East: Solace; great spirituality; contemplation. You will find success unexpectedly.

In the South: The emergence of new ideas; regeneration of spirit; renewed fervour. Creative inspiration. Zest; a desire to rebuild. Mental strength.

In the West: The uncovering of deception; the unmasking of fraud. Those who had been secretly working against you will be found out.

In the North: Recognition of your abilities and gifts from those in authority. Recompense and gratitude.

4 Bamboo, 4 Circles, 7 Circles   TREASURE   (Pao) 寶

By industry are gathered together the precious possessions. A sure reward for services; material gains through an unexpected source. The appearance of 'Treasure' in the East indicates that the questioner has a fund of talents and assets which he may not be putting to his fullest use. By thinking about what action he might take, he will be able to realize these assets, or use his talents to his better advantage.

5 Bamboo, 8 Circles   WISDOM   (Chih) 智

The Tiger guards the Lotus. Strength and Wisdom are combined together. In the West, this combination indicates material gains through industriousness. In other sectors, it indicates the achieving of Wisdom. It is a sign of protection of the innocent, or a guard over treasure — if one has valuable things, it is wise to keep them well guarded.

Other Associations

With the Duck, 2 Bamboo, it indicates satisfaction and companionship; contended neighbours; geniality.

―――――――――――――   ●   ―――――――――――――

6 Bamboo   WATER   (Shui) 水

GRATITUDE — CONTINUATION — WISDOM — FERTILITY

Guardian: Bamboo

With Guardian: A Book

Secondary meaning: Water and Bamboo; words flow like Water, with Bamboo they are written and recorded.

Commentary

The highest good is that of water. Without water there is no life; its goodness benefits a myriad creatures, yet itself it does not aspire to attain heights. It flows from the highest peaks to the deepest valleys; there it stays and becomes even. Water is one of the Five Elements, the other four being wood, fire, earth, and metal. Water is produced by metal, and itself produces wood (that is, dew collects on metal objects at night; water enters plants and is turned into wood). Water is destroyed (polluted) by earth, and itself quenches fire. The qualities of water are life-bringing; abundance and fertility are its attributes.

Cities are built on the shores of the sea, and near rivers, because water is found there; hence, towns and cities are represented by water. Water flows and continues, therefore, in questions of romance, water does not signify constancy. Water signifies fertility and abundance, therefore in questions of business matters water shows benefits. Water is vital to life, therefore in matters of health water signifies recovery.

Water in conflict with wind produces storms; therefore in the North, where there are winds, it signifies conflicts. Water and earth together make clay, therefore with 3 Wan, Earth, it signifies building and development. The Chinese character for calamity combines the characters for fire and water; 6 Bamboo and 6 Wan in opposite sectors indicate disaster or accident. 1 Wan symbolizes Man, and this tile in association with Water may shows stress.

Chung tile:	The symbol is of water which has flowed from the peaks into a receptacle or reservoir. Here there is stillness; contentment; gratitude.
First tile:	Water as the first tile shows continuation of what is good; flowing downstream to greater abundance.
Last tile:	Water as the last tile shows turmoil; it is an indication of conflict, of violent energy. It may mean upheaval; guard against the unexpected.
In the East:	This shows water beginning on its journey downstream. It shows the need to pursue ideals; to follow ideas through; to keep a check on expenditure.
In the South:	Water in the South shows great abundance and flourishing fields. It shows the beneficial outcome of business projects; returns from investments.
In the West:	Water in the West indicates writing; correspondence; studies; learning and teaching. It indicates the accumulation of knowledge.

In the North: The North symbolizes winter and storms; there will be conflict; but from the conflict there will come strength.

6 Bamboo, 6 Circles   HEALTH   (K'ang) 康

Water is with the Peach Tree, representing the vital essences. It signifies health, and recovery from diseases of circulation or where fluids in the body are concerned. Water and the Peach in the North indicate mental illness, and the successful recovery from stress and agitation. In the West, it indicates the recovery from illness of someone who is closely related to the questioner. In certain other questions, it means fertility and fecundity; it relates to the birth of a new baby; it indicates large families.

6 Bamboo, 3 Wan   ABUNDANCE   (Ch'ang) 昌

Water and Earth together make clay. It indicates building, cities, new estates, development of projects; success and prosperity through building. It indicates busy trade, and the growth of commerce. It shows return for investment in construction or traffic.

6 Bamboo, 6 Wan   PROGRESS   (Chin) 進

Fire is quenched by Water; the significance will vary according to the sector in which Fire and Water appear. It may indicate conflict, but in the North, where Water and Wind indicate conflict, the conflict is lessened by the action of Fire and Water. Where the question refers to illness, Fire and Water is symbolic of the passing of the illness, and the successful recovery of the patient. In questions of business, there may be losses and eventual recovery. Fire and Water indicate change and progress.

——————————— • ———————————

7 Bamboo TORTOISE (Kuei)

THOUGHT — CHASTITY — INTUITION — UBIQUITY

Guardian: Winter

With Guardian: An Old Man
Secondary meaning: The personage of an Old Man indicates dignity and
                     respect.

Commentary

The tortoise is the symbol of the Universe; the dome of its back represents the vault of Heaven. The tortoise is one of the Four Fabulous Beasts, and is in its realm in the North. The Black Tortoise is the symbol of the Northern Sector of the Heavens. The tortoise carapace was used in ancient times for divination, being touched with a hot iron, and the resultant cracks studied. The diagrams of the I Ching were, according to legend, found inscribed on the back of a tortoise, as was the Lo Shu, or Lo River Magic Square. By virtue of its longevity, the tortoise is a sign of long life, old age, sagacity, and memory. It is the bearer of memorial tablets, and hence the conveyor of sad news. It is the symbol of thought, for it was formerly believed that tortoises could only conceive by the power of thought: hence the tortoise meant chastity. In the same way, a child whose father was not known was euphemistically said to have a tortoise for a father. Hence, can signify a child without a father.

The tortoise represents the power to see into the future; the bearing of sad news; chastity; intuition; the powers of the brain. Because of its association with the numbers of the magic square, the Tortoise can indicate success in mathematics and accountancy.

In matters of the heart, it is better to be wise; for the Tortoise indicates both chastity and illegitimacy. In matters of health, the Tortoise indicates old age and active memory. In business, the Tortoise, symbolizing the Universe, indicates world trade. The professions associated with the Tortoise are accountancy and gerontology.

Chung tile: Progress may seem slow at present, but success is
                    assured with perseverance.

First tile: The Tortoise in the first place does not indicate
                       success for those wishing to make a new start, for
                       there will be delays and initial set-backs. However,
                       once the foundations are laid, progress will be on a
                       firm footing.

Last tile: Present business will endure; there is a firm found-
                       ation and consolidation of effort. The Tortoise in its
                       Realm indicates long-term benefits.

In the East: The Tortoise in the East symbolizes the Sun em-
                       barking on its journey across the sky; there is a great
                       distance to travel; there is much work to be done,
                       and little will be achieved by trying to hurry matters.

In the South: The Tortoise opposite its realm indicates worldwide
                       communications; long distances; expansion. It
                       reminds the questioner of all the many details that
                       go to make up the question; that matters are not as
                       simple as the questioner would like them to be.

In the West: This sector indicates old age; respect due to an elder;
                       grandparents. It warns the questioner not to forget
                       his responsibilities.

In the North: Memory; reminiscences. Books, diaries, and
                       histories.

7 Bamboo   MEMORY   (*See* **North**)

———————————— • ————————————

8 Bamboo   MUSHROOMS   (Chün)

VIRTUE – IMMORTALITY – MANNA – ECCENTRICITY

Guardian: Autumn

With Guardian: A Boat

Secondary meaning: Mushrooms are the only vegetables which float on
                      water, hence they signify the crossing of a stream.

Commentary

The mushroom is the plant of immortality; it is the food which is provided by Heaven, whereas other food is provided by the Earth. The mushroom only grows during the times of virtuous rulers, hence it is a sign of virtuous conduct and correct action. Its unfamiliarity signifies unconventional conduct, eccentric behaviour, extraordinary events. It indicates aliens, strangers, foreigners, strange objects, and the unusual or erratic.

In matters of the heart, it indicates an unusual alliance or relationship, or a union with someone of a totally different background. In business it indicates extraordinary undertakings, the branching out into hitherto unexplored or strange fields. In matters of health, it indicates unconventional medicine. In the career field, it indicates an unusual means of earning a living; the realms of the exotic or adventurous. The mushroom flourishes in the autumn, which is indicated by the West. In the Spring, indicated by East, it remains hidden. In the winter, shown by North, it has already disappeared.

Chung tile:	An extraordinary event will take you by surprise. An unexpected proposition.
First tile:	Strange ideas are presented; they will eventually result in success, but the present time is not ripe.
Last tile:	That which has gone is only hidden.
In the East:	The time is not yet ripe for the projects in hand; however, they will come to fruition unexpectedly.
In the South:	This indicates a meeting with a stranger; at first, his proposals will seem strange and bizarre, but in time his meaning will become clear.
In the West:	Strange events bring unexpected successes. The time is ripe for projects of a new and untried nature; one should not be afraid to try new directions.
In the North:	Irregular events which were thought to have been settled have only been put to one side. The strange events of the last few months will recur.

8 Bamboo, 5 Wan   KNOWLEDGE   (Chih) 知

Mushrooms by a house indicates virtue entering the house. It indicates a well-run household, or business. There will be success through correct procedures, and attention to details. A peaceful family content within the home. Knowledge and experience; wisdom through virtue.

Also **8 Bamboo, 7 Circles**

The Mushroom and the Insect signify virtue and industry; reward and success through sustained effort.

──────────────────   •   ──────────────────

9 Bamboo   THE WILLOW TREE   (Yang) 楊

RETICENCE – MILDNESS – TEMPERANCE – MODESTY

Guardian: Bamboo

With Guardian: A River

Secondary meaning: The willow and the bamboo grow by the water, and they signify a river; it is wide and long, and signifies a long and arduous journey.

Commentary

The willow tree, drooping its head, indicates modest behaviour; being able to resist the onslaught of the North winds, it shows endurance and fortitude in the face of adversity. 'Winds there may be that please only the willow.' The character for willow shows a tree, and at the side the character yang, which is similar to that for the 'I' of I Ching, showing that its osiers may have been used once for divining stalks. The ninth tile of the suits signifies the Nine Felicitations or Similitudes: the mountains and hills, greater and lesser heights, streams in all directions, the constancy of the Moon, the rising of the Sun, the longevity of the Southern mountain, and the luxuriance of the evergreen trees.

   In affairs of the heart, the Willow signifies courtship; in business, successful dealings, and the ability to maintain progress in the face of opposition. In matters of health, it signifies recovery through the taking of certain medicines. Of the professions, it indicates travel, or overseas trade.

Chung tile: The Willow in the central place indicates satisfaction in the winter.

First tile: The Willow as the first tile signifies modesty; it may be advantageous to show people your true worth; your talents may be unrecognized.

Last tile: The Willow in the last place shows the ability to overcome obstacles through personal fortitude. It is a sign that present troubles will soon pass if borne with patience.

In the East: The Willow blossoming in the spring is one of the first welcome sights after winter: it indicates joy, and success after a stagnant period.

In the South: The Willow in its full greenery by the river shows contentment; the river indicates travel. There will be occasion for great rejoicing.

In the West: Mildness and virtue; steadfastness in adversity. There will be occasions for regrets for the wrongdoings of others. Longing.

In the North: Fortitude and endurance; the ability to account for one's actions to those in authority. Success after considerable stress.

9 Bamboo, 2 Circles, 6 Circles   THREE TREES   (Shen) 森

The Three Trees, Willow, Peach and the Pine, indicate the trees of all seasons; the willow of spring, the peach of summer, and the pine of winter. They indicate success, progress, and continuation of projects. The Three Trees symbolize forests: hence, abundance; a good harvest; stored-up wealth; good fortune.

Also 9 Bamboo-North   STRENGTH   (*See* North)

——————————— ● ———————————

(vi) THE CIRCLE TILES

The Circle is a very ancient symbol, being the emblem of the solar (or lunar) disc and the sign of Heaven itself. Heaven was held to be round, the earth square, and this symbolism can be seen in the diviner's plate (the Shih (式)), also certain circular bronze mirrors which have a square design at their centre, and even in the strings of Chinese coins called 'cash'. The concept of the Cycle — the inevitability of the seasons, the rise and setting of the Sun, death and rebirth — fascinated early Chinese philosophers, and was embodied by them in the Yin and Yang concept of Change and Constancy. Jade discs, called Pi, were used in Chinese rituals even in archaic times. The jade itself was mined in Siberia, where they were made into circular or semi-circular shapes (even into split ring shapes), and delicately engraved with stylized patterns. Sometimes the edges of the discs were carved into highly formal animal shapes. They were highly prized as currency and laid behind and at each side of the head of a powerful king when he was laid out for burial, but strangely enough, the ancient Chinese writers seemed uncertain of their purpose. Modern scholarship has shown that these carved discs may at one time have had an astronomical purpose and that they were used as a kind of template for sighting certain constellations in the sky, and hence determine the seasons of the year. However, by the time the sacred rites were drawn up their original purpose was forgotten, although it was known that they were formerly held in great veneration. (They were, after all, highly sophisticated astronomical instruments, which must have taken a lifetime — if not lifetimes — to calibrate.)

Now, the circle represents coinage — tokens of wealth and possession. For some people, the token is sufficient — money is all. The Chinese term for Circle tiles is T'ung (筒), which means conduit pipe or tube when written with the 'bamboo' radical, the usual way (in Chinese manuals) of indicating the Circle tiles. This is clearly an orthographical error, for (筒) refers to that cylindrical nature of a tube which is its length. The character should be (銅) which means brass or bronze, hence a brass coin. However, the usage of T'ung (筒) may have originated in the fortune-teller's K'o T'ung (課筒) or Examining Tube.

The Circle tiles are the central rank in the twenty-seven suit tiles. Their engravings show more variety of colour than the Bamboo tiles (which are predominantly green) and the Wan tiles (which are all red and black). Four of the Circle tiles are perfect: 1 — Peacock, 3 — Phoenix, 5 — Dragon, and 9 — Unicorn; two pairs are impure: 2 — Pine, and 4 — Jade; and one tile, 8 — Tiger, is pure black, the only pure black tile in all the suit tiles. It will be recalled that the Cardinal Points are the only other pure black tiles, and that Chung (Centre) is the only pure red tile among all the tiles in the Mah Jongg set.

This range of colour combinations is a significant contrast to the stable greens of the bamboo tiles. The imbalance of the two-colour (impure) tiles striving to divide up and go separate ways, or else acquire the missing third colour, demonstrates change, movement, agitation, unexpected events, personality clashes and strong ambition. While the two-colour tiles show conflict and upheaval, the three-colour (perfect) tiles symbolize power in confidence, and harnessable force. The black tile (Tiger) represents a very powerful force which can work in opposition or agreement depending on its place, and its associating tiles.

The Circle tiles indicate people of commerce and trade; people who are concerned with the everyday practicalities of the business of living in a tangible but unpredictable world.

1 Circle   PEARL   (Chu) 珠

REFINEMENT — FINESSE — HONOUR — FIDELITY

Guardians: Orchid

With Guardian: Protection

Secondary meaning: The pearl and orchid indicate refined possessions; something prized for its beauty rather than intrinsic value.

Commentary

1 Circle is one of the three tiles among the suits which has a special significance in the game of Mah Jongg; under certain conditions, winning with the 1 Circle is known as 'Fishing the Moon from the Bottom of the Sea'. The Moon refers to the disc, 1 Circle, marked on the tile, but it can also mean, figuratively, something precious; pearls are jewels which are taken from the bottom of the sea. The symbolism of the pearl is fidelity even to the death, chastity and honour. It indicates

protection against fire (because of its association with water) and is held to have curative properties; ground up pearls were mixed with wine and drunk as an expensive medicine. Indicating refinement, it also shows excellence in literary composition. The Pearl and the Peacock (1 Bamboo) together indicate vanity. In matters of the heart, the Pearl indicates love of beauty; shallow romantic love. In matters of business, it indicates successes through speculation in the fine arts; in the professions it indicates the fine arts and jewellery, antiques and *objets de vertu*. In matters of health it indicates wasted expense on costly treatment, when more homely remedies would have sufficed.

Chung tile: The Pearl in the Chung place foretells a small but unexpected financial gain; it also indicates that something may be of greater value than had been estimated. Hidden values.

First tile: The Pearl in the first place refers to the questioner and indicates honour and refinement. It is necessary to honour an agreement.

Last tile: The Pearl in the last place is an indication of unexpected reward; a lucky chance; a sudden announcement that will bring benefits.

In the East: The Pearl in the East indicates the signing of an agreement; it indicates a financial transaction of an important nature, and it is necessary to examine the details carefully.

In the South: The Pearl indicates the Sun and Moon shining together; promotion and advancement. It is an indication that some things may be of greater value than had been realized; it may be important to reassess one's assets.

In the West: The Pearl in the West indicates fire — danger by fire is possible. It shows precious things in jeopardy, but the outcome will not be excessive loss.

In the North: The Pearl in the North shows refinement in the arts; it indicates proficiency in the spoken word — words

like pearls — but there is a danger of heeding to
flattering admirers.

——————————   •   ——————————

2 Circles   PINE

(Sung)

RENEWED STRENGTH — RENEWED YOUTH — INTEGRITY — ATTACHMENT

Guardian: Winter

With Guardian: Tree of Life (or Old Woman)

Secondary meaning: An old woman with a stick; she strikes the ground
and a tree springs up. It is the Tree of Life,
inaccessible to mortals, rejuvenating and re-
animating when its cones are eaten. The branches
are arranged in three pairs, with three cones on each
branch, and three more cones at the top.

Commentary

The pine is evergreen, and hence indicates long life and faithfulness. At
the side of the pine tree, an old woman sits and reminisces, but does not
count the years. The pine is one of the Nine Felicitous Similitudes
described under 9 Bamboo: 'May you flourish as the Pine and Cypress'
indicates constancy. The pine and chrysanthemum are both signs of
endurance, for they flourish in winter. The pine and willow are planted
by tombs and graveyards, and are therefore significant of sorrow. The
Pine and Fire (6 Wan) indicate danger by fire. The Pine and Plum
indicate friendship. The Pine and Bamboo indicate moral integrity: firm
and enduring like the Pine Tree, resistant and as unassailable as the
bamboo's skin.

The Pine indicates sternness, rectitude, discipline, tenacity, and
strong attachment and loyalty. In matters of the heart, it indicates a long
and lasting relationship. In business affairs, it shows strong progress and
success; in medical matters it shows ability to withstand disease, and to
recover from a severe illness. Of the trades and professions, the Pine,
because its wood was burnt to make the finest carbon-black for ink,
indicates a connection with printing, publishing, and the manufacture
of books and stationery materials.

Chung tile: There will be opposition, but with strength and determination you will have eventual success.

First tile: The Pine as the first tile indicates a strong will, determination, and the ability to get things done. It shows tenacity and perseverance.

Last tile: As the last tile, the Pine shows renewed vigour; stamina, an ability to carry on when others have given up. Success through perseverance.

In the East: This indicates opposition and danger, but a successful outcome through perseverance.

In the South: This indicates thrusting forward; vigour; progress; physical strength. Matters will be able to go ahead as planned.

In the West: This indicates renewed vigour in old age; the revitalizing of old ideas; the re-establishment of something which had been long forgotten.

In the North: 'Stern as the swift wind in the pines'. This indicates discipline, firm authority, and determination.

2 Circles, 9 Bamboo, 6 Circles   THREE TREES   (*See* **9 Bamboo**)

───────────────   ●   ───────────────

3 Circles   PHOENIX   (Fêng) 鳳

JOY — HAPPINESS — SPLENDOUR — MAGNIFICENCE

Guardian: Summer

With Guardian: The Sun

Secondary meaning: The brilliance of the Sun at midday, or the splendid phoenix in summer, indicates imperial power.

Commentary

The phoenix is one of the Four Fabulous Beasts; it is a sign of the Emperor. It invariably indicated a good omen; numerous expressions of felicity include the phoenix and its attributes: a complimentary expression to a high official was to compare his son with the plumage of the phoenix — a worthy attribute. The resting phoenix was a sign that goodness would be rewarded. The appearance of the phoenix was a good omen, since it only appeared as a mythical bird in so far that it was the subject of numerous legends, it may originally have been an actual bird, such as the golden pheasant, in the same way that the unicorn may have had its origins in tales of the rhinoceros. (The phoenix of Chinese legend, Feng, is not identical to the phoenix of the Arabian nights, since the Chinese phoenix existed in male and female forms: indeed there are separate words for the male and female phoenix. There is no Chinese legend regarding its building a nest and setting fire to it, for example.)

The phoenix may be identified with the Vermilion Bird — one of the four Heavenly Palaces of Chinese astronomy. It indicates the Southern part of the heavens, in the same way that the Phoenix is said to be in its Realm when it is in association with South, or in the South sector. Vermilion is the colour of the Emperor, who always sealed and wrote in red. In the North, the Phoenix faces the South, also a good omen; the beneficial portents of the Phoenix are not lessened by its being in the sector opposite its realm. However, in association with a North tile, the same auspicious omen is not inferred. The Phoenix indicates the giving of a daughter in marriage; it also indicates classical music. It therefore blends harmoniously with the Lute tile, 4 Wan. The emblem also represents eminence in other ways; through literary pursuits or scholarship. The Phoenix is used to refer to devoted sons; those who support their parents. It is, because of its brilliant plumage, the symbol of a handsome young man.

In matters of the heart, it may signify the marriage of a daughter, or engagement to a handsome young man of good family. In business matters, it indicates prosperity. In health, it shows recovery. In the professions, it indicates music and the theatre.

Chung tile: The Phoenix in the Chung position indicates great financial reward. Matters will proceed better than expected. Hopes will be realized.

First tile: The Phoenix in the first place shows great joy and happiness; it may be through a marriage or new relationship; prosperity is shown.

Last tile:	The Phoenix in the last place indicates the prospects of a young man, looking out into the future. There are fortunate indications; great optimism.
In the East:	The Phoenix in the East shows the Imperial bird growing in splendour under the rising Sun. It shows the commencement of a long journey, or the embarkation on a prosperous undertaking. It also indicates Royal approbation.
In the South:	Great prosperity is shown by the Phoenix in its own realm, the South, the mansion of the Sun. It shows fortune, increasing opportunities, and valuable connections.
In the West:	The Phoenix does not leave its Imperial perch; this is one of two proverbs taken to mean meddlesome behaviour. The Phoenix does not leave its perch to meddle in mortal matters; why should you want to busy yourself with outside affairs.
In the North:	The Phoenix facing the Sun, and rejoicing. A good omen. For those connected with the performing arts, it indicates great success. For those wishing to marry, it indicates a successful match.

3 Circles-South PROSPERITY   (*See* **South**)

——————————————— ● ———————————————

4 Circles JADE   (Yü) 玉

ROYALTY — VALUE — RESISTANCE — WORTH

Guardian:	Bamboo
With Guardian:	The Bell
Secondary meaning:	The Stone Chime was a standard pitch; being made of stone it did not slacken like the strings of the lute, nor become worn like the metal bell. Hence, it

signified an absolute standard, reliability,
correctness.

Commentary

Whereas the phoenix is concerned with the visible attributes of Imperial
power — splendour, magnificence, and all its outer show — jade is the
symbol of royalty and authority. Jade was regarded as the symbol of
royal authority since the earliest times; reference has already been made
to the stone Pi at the beginning of the section on the Circle tiles. Yet
before it is polished and fashioned, jade is worthless: it appears as a dull
green stone and would not be valued but for the workmanship which
went into converting the hard and almost unyielding stone into an
ornament of beauty. Jade is therefore intrinsically valueless; it is the
attribution of man's efforts which change the rough jade into something
precious. Similarly, it is only by good government that those in power
are valued. An unjust ruler has no value at all.

Jade also indicates a strong and talented young man. Because of its
hardness, Jade may indicate hard-heartedness, resistance, difficulties
and displeasure. Jade with the Orchid indicates precious things. It is a
sign of authority; it shows judgement. Because it takes so long to fashion,
it indicates long effort and hard work.

In matters of the heart, it indicates the meeting with a strong, young
man. But it shows hard-heartedness; there is no response in this case. In
matters of business, it shows difficulties; existing prospects are enduring,
but it is hard to break new ground. In matters of health, it shows
resistance to disease. It indicates immunization; where the question is of
health, and Jade appears in a Northerly or Westerly area, it indicates the
taking of precautions. In matters of a career, Jade indicates the legal
profession.

Chung tile:	You may need to make a greater effort, or outlay, than you anticipated, but the results will be worthwhile.
First tile:	You will need to make a careful decision which you will not enjoy; what you may want immediately may not be the best in the end. Be just and firm.
Last tile:	Unyielding authority will not accede to your request. Constant effort must be brought to bear in order to succeed.

In the East: A favourable decision by authority. A letter of introduction.

In the South: A document which will help to solve problems; a meeting with someone in authority.

In the West: Conflict with authority; hardship. A request turned down.

In the North: Difficulties and obstinacy. Progress halted.

4 Circles-Centre ESTEEM   (*See* **Centre**)

4 Circles, 5 Bamboo, 7 Circles TREASURE   (*See* **5 Bamboo**)

———————————————— • ————————————————

5 Circles DRAGON   (Lung) 龍

FLATTERY — CUNNING — OBSCURITY — MALICE

Guardian: Spring

With Guardian: A Carriage

Secondary meaning: The Dragon is seen pulling the Heavenly Chariot. The indications are of fire, speed, and rapid change. It indicates a summons: the modern meaning is a journey by air. Rapid change.

Supplementary reading: A rich man owned a carriage; a poor neighbour, whose mother had died, wished to borrow the carriage for the funeral, but was too much in awe of the rich man to ask. Later, the rich man heard of this, and was distressed. Because the carriage could not be used when it was most required he had the carriage buried. Significance: there are those who wish to help but are unaware that their assistance is needed.

Commentary

The dragon is one of the most universal emblems in Chinese mythology, folklore, and philosophy. It is tied up in many ways with widely different areas of thought; not just as a mythical beast, but as a potent force in Nature. Through its association with Imperial power, the dragon signifies strength, magnaminity, protection. In mythology and astrology the dragon is associated with craft, cunning, wisdom, dexterity. The concept of the dragon devouring the Sun or the Moon at the time of eclipse indicates a demanding nature; the eclipse also indicates obscurity, loss, theft.

Because of the many aspects of the dragon, it is best to regard the Dragon tile as an omniphagous one, and interpret an arrangement of tiles in the light of the Dragon having swallowed up the tiles around it. The Dragon has to be considered numerically. As the centre tile of the central rank of the three suits, 5 Circles represents the central point of the Lo Shu, or Magic Squares which radiate in all directions. 5 Circles therefore represents the Centre; indeed, it is almost more central than the Chung tile itself, for Chung, the Central Cardinal Point, only represents the Centre, or present, on Earth, while 5 Circles represents the Centre in all directions; not just to the eight points of the compass, but the twenty-six directions, above, below, and the remaining points. (It is advisable to refer to the section on the Lo Shu in the first part of this book, p. 49.) The appearance of 5 Circles in any triad of tiles must be regarded in respect to the numerical relationship of the tiles either side. If the total is 42, it indicates extreme good fortune; if 15, it shows success. (The numerical interpretation of the 5 Circles tile outweighs the secondary importance of its function as a Dragon tile; if there is no numerical result, the tile can be read according to the symbolic meanings.) The 5 Circle tile is one of the three suit tiles which have a special significance in the game of Mah Jongg; in certain cases it is referred to as 'plum blossom on the roof'. Therefore, with the Plum tile it becomes a fortunate association, and indicates sudden prosperity, or good fortune in other matters.

The colour of the dragon is sky blue; and its proper region in the East. The appearance of the Dragon in the East is therefore a fortunate sign, indicating sudden change for the better, the kind of change depending on the tiles which the Dragon has 'swallowed'. The Dragon and the Tortoise (7 Bamboo) indicate the forces of Yin and Yang combined, and so indicate a union. The Imperial emblematic creatures, the Phoenix (3 Circles) and the Dragon together indicate success in literary fields; they may signify the passing of examinations, or success with cultural pursuits.

It is difficult to give interpretations of the Dragon tile on its own without knowing the associating tiles, but generally the following prospects are indicated. In matters of romance, examine the associating tiles to see which kind of symbols have been swallowed. If they are indicative of the questioner, then it signifies the questioner being swallowed up by the romance itself, leading to heartache. In matters of business, it indicates a merger, and very fast turn-over.

In matters of health, it indicates speedy recovery from disease through surgery. In career matters, it indicates restlessness and dissatisfaction with anything that means staying in one place for long. Careers which involve travel and change are best.

The Dragon is also an indication of rain and floods, and may act as a warning against flood damage, especially if associated with the River, Stream, or Water tiles.

Chung tile: The appearance of 5 Circles as the Chung tile is a sign of certain fortune. The Dragon indications are of sudden opportunity, which must be grasped because it will be of short duration.

First tile: There is flattery and malice; be on your guard against cunning.

Last tile: There is an indication of the need to act quickly, since opportunities are only of short duration.

In the East: The Blue Dragon is in its realm in the East. This is a good portent; examine the tiles either side; if they indicate positive and beneficial aspects, the Dragon will strengthen the indications. If there are negative aspects, the Dragon will ward off the malign influences.

In the South: The indication here is of travel, extreme agitation, frantic activity. It also recalls the proverb 'The Dragon does not love to leave its pool' — an indication of a busybody. Activity, movement, unexpected journeys.

In the West: The Dragon is opposite to the Tiger; there will be conflict of interests; there is an indication of

trickery; of slander, malice and gossip. One should
be on one's guard against fawning flatterers; the
dragon's aspects (alertness, astuteness) need to be
used to the full to ward off impending danger
through disguised enemies.

In the North: The activity of the Dragon is lessened when in the
domain of the Tortoise; the indications here are of
merging, union, joining. Change, but strength
through the addition of new resources.

5 Circles-East BENEVOLENCE ●   (*See* East)

---------------- ● ----------------

6 Circles PEACH   (T'ao) 桃

BEAUTY — LUXURY — PROFLIGACY — INDULGENCE — MARRIAGE

Guardian: Summer

With Guardian: The Fan

Secondary meaning: A courtesan holds a fan to her face; it indicates
luxury, leisure, idleness; also, a neglected wife.

Commentary
The peach is a sign of feminine beauty; images of the peach, and others
made of peach wood, are made to trap evil spirits. When the Dowager
Empress of the West visited the emperor she brought him seven peaches;
they were so delicious that he said he would grow them; she was amused,
for the heavenly peaches were from a tree that blossomed only once
every three thousand years: the tree of immortality. The elixir of life is
distilled from peach stones and made by the toad in the moon.

The symbolism of peaches meaning feminine beauty is not confined to
China; the delicate colours, the fragrance, the soft touch, the velvety
skin have all been used as metaphors of feminine charms. By extension,
the symbolism of the peach signifies laziness, or indulgence. The
Chinese version of Arcadia, the Shangri-La of legend, was discovered by
a scholar wandering through a peach forest, where he met a race of

people who knew nothing of the wars and tribulations in the outside world. By extension, the peach forest signifies a refuge from persecution; sanctuary, and seclusion. With a 2 of any suit, or a double 6 Circles, the indication is of two beauties, and hence, rivalry, quarrels, and strife; jealousy.

The beauty that is depicted by the Peach is not of the enduring kind; in matters of the heart the Peach indicates youthful romance; a passing fancy; indiscretion. It can indicate wantonness and profligacy; wasteful spending. In matters of business, it indicates the need to keep a sharper eye on finances, to cut down on needless expenditure, and to avoid unnecessary show. In matters of health, it indicates a delicate constitution, and illness of the abdomen. In other respects, it signifies sound health. Peach also refers to feminine intuition, and with the Toad (3 Bamboo) it signifies the ability to cut through a problem with quick-wittedness.

Chung tile: It is easy to fall into idle ways. The opportunities for self-indulgence are numbered; be warned against extravagance.

First tile: An opportunity for indulgence and enjoyment; a short-lived romantic affair.

Last tile: Be warned against the dangers of profligacy; avoid the temptation to squander on leisure.

In the East: This is a sign of youthful relationships; it indicates gaiety, and many social engagements. Opportunities for meeting new friends.

In the South: A sign of over-indulgence; more play than work; a tendency to over-spend: although on the positive side, it indicates that the opportunities to do so may have yet to present themselves.

In the West: Jealousy and quarrels; infidelity. Mistrust through selfishness. Neglect of duty, lack of loyalty.

In the North: A need to reconsider present actions; danger from an associate; professional jealousy. Espionage.

6 Circles, 6 Bamboo   HEALTH   (*See* **6 Bamboo**)

6 Circles, 2 Circles, 9 Bamboo   THREE TREES   (*See* **9 Bamboo**)

●

7 Circles   INSECT   (Ch'ung)

CRAFT — SKILL — TECHNIQUE — INDUSTRY

Guardian: Chrysanthemum

With Guardian: Prevarication

Secondary meaning: Sages arguing over trifles, unconcerned with real issues.

Commentary

The Insect, meaning the industrious insects such as the ant, the silk-worm, and the bee, signifies work, technical skill, and craft. It indicates progress in all affairs to do with manual labour. It signifies the fitting of houses, the making of furniture, the weaving of cloth, the making of things. The Insect shows the workpeople getting on with their tasks unconcerned with the passage of political events, family squabbles or other affairs. It can show irritation (especially with 2 Wan) with those who frustrate efforts; the sting of a bee or wasp is ready to strike those that interfere with what it considers to be its duty. With Yin tiles, or tiles which indicate scholarly pursuits, it shows too much attention to trifles; arguments over finer details. It consistently shows the subject being involved in the work in progress, not being distracted by outside interests, but possibly over-punctilious in attention to detail; but this is because the work is a source of pride. The work is the end; not the means to earning a living.

   In matters of romance, it indicates a working relationship; two people of similar interests who both share concern for their work. In business, it indicates excellent progress for those involved in manufacturing; in matters of health, it shows the subject being too preoccupied with work to be worried about health matters — industrial diseases are the danger. All trades, and skills, engineering, production, are indicated by Insect.

Chung tile: 'Chung' Centre, and 'Ch'ung' Insect, are almost homophones; even the written characters are similar. The indication is of great pride in one's work; there will be ample reward for one's industries; great satisfaction.

First tile: The Insect in the first place is a sign of high quality craftsmanship; an attention to detail; the avoidance of distraction. There will be great satisfaction; reward and recognition.

Last tile: The industrious will continue to make progress. Though the rewards may seem slight, there will be satisfaction in the result.

In the East: Fine craftsmanship, high standards, attention to detail, enthusiasm for one's work, a sense of responsibility and industry are shown by the Insect in this quarter. There will be considerable achievement.

In the South: The Insect in the summer indicates considerable activity; there may be busy competition, and quarrels, but they will not be of a lasting nature.

In the West: Over-attention to detail is the fault shown by the sages arguing over a trifle in the autumn, while amused workers go about their day-to-day business. It is important to pay attention to the realities of life; academic answers do not solve the questions of daily living.

In the North: Satsfaction, though the rewards may be meagre. Financial gain is less important than pride in one's work.

7 Circles, 5 Bamboo, 4 Circles TREASURE   (*See* **5 Bamboo**)

8 Circles   TIGER   (Hu)

BRAVERY – PROWESS – VIRILITY – CRUELTY

Guardian: Autumn

With Guardian: A Bridge

Secondary meaning: Although the tiger is regarded as embodying the masculine attributes, it is unexpectedly also regarded as having Yin properties; the tiger can be seen as the bridge between ideas (Heaven) and mankind (Earth).

Commentary

The attributes of the tiger are fierceness, prowess, authority. The tiger can frighten into submission; it indicates strength. Valour and strength are the requirements of wisdom. The tiger shows a dangerous situation. The foolish man will try and catch a tiger by holding on to its tail. It indicates a dangerous situation which one finds difficult to get out of: 'He who rides a tiger will find it difficult to dismount.' It signifies opposition in the face of determination; in the North, the opposition to plans is indicated strong, determining tiles in the South. But 'A man who genuinely desires to understand the truth will give his body to a tiger.' The problems may look daunting, but they may not be as bad as they seem: 'The bare hide of the tiger is like the bare hide of a sheep.' The tiger is a furry animal; furry animals are regarded as Yin, and so the Tiger, for all its fierceness and strength, is able to embody Yin and Yang properties together — hence the secondary significance of a bridge. In the case of a female questioner, it indicates the possession of the qualities which are traditionally considered masculine: physical bravery, stamina, practical determination. It may indicate a person who has to support a family; it may show someone having to fight for their rights. It indicates aggressiveness, but not belligerence for its own sake.

The White Tiger is one of the quarters of the Heavens, representing the West, and therefore the West is where Tiger shows its most powerful influences. The splendid coat of the tiger indicates masculine vanity; it indicates a vain, or extrovert streak.

It is said that when a tiger eats a man, the man's spirit becomes the tiger's assistant; therefore, a person eaten by a tiger is someone who panders to evil-doers; one who abets or connives at a crime. Underhand dealings are shown by the appearance of the Tiger in the North.

In matters of romance, the Tiger indicates a fiery relationship, one which will be marked by blazing quarrels, arguments, and bouts of temper. It shows a love-hate relationship in which both sides are continually battling. There will be walk-outs, reconciliations, and a repeat of the cycle until the somewhat unsatisfactory partnership is finally broken up. In matters of business, it is a case of the stronger side winning; one should not be overawed by the strength of the competition, but one should not allow the other side to gain the advantage.

In matters of health, it indicates wounds and fevers. The West indicates the illness at its height; the South that it is passing; the East that it is still progressing.

The profession indicated by the Tiger is a military one; the armed forces, the police, or the other uniformed services.

Chung tile: There will be strong opposition to your proposals. It is necessary to seize any opportunity to gain the advantage.

First tile: The first tile indicates personal valour; but the remaining interpretations of this tile may signify opposition, since the East is opposite to the Tiger's domain.

Last tile: The Tiger is in the domain of the Tortoise; this indicates being extricated from a difficult situation.

In the East: The East is connected with the questioner; it is the opposite domain to that of the Tiger; hence here the negative qualities of the Tiger are shown. An overbearing nature; male vanity; cruelty (which may be in the sense of teasing or nagging). Opposition to plans by those in a position to exert influence through authority or wealth.

In the South: The South shows the benign influence of the Tiger at work; it shows the assistance from a powerful ally, or the subject using his authority to cut down scheming opposition.

In the West:	The Tiger is strongest in his domain. It shows powerful authority, and strength which can be called upon. Valour is one of the requirements of Wisdom.
In the North:	The Tiger's influences are lessened by the more lethargic processes of the Tortoise. If there is opposition, it may be swept away by delaying tactics.

8 Circles-White   WHITE TIGER   (*See* White)

8 Circles, Centre, 4 Bamboo   VALOUR   (*See* Centre)

———————————————— • ————————————————

9 Circles   UNICORN   (Ch'i) 麒

SHARPNESS — ACUITY — WONDER — INGENUITY

Guardian:	Plum
With Guardian:	A Well
Secondary meaning:	A man digs a well in order that a unicorn can drink; some sacrifices will need to be made in order that you can carry out your purpose. The end justifies the means.

Commentary

The unicorn was believed to be one of the four supernatural beasts which appeared in time of just government. It had the body of a deer, the tail of an ox, the hooves of a horse; it had variegated colours on its back, and its belly was yellow. It neither trod on grass, nor ate anything. The Japanese have adapted the character for unicorn to mean the giraffe, which neatly fits this description. Today, the rhinoceros is believed to be the unicorn, and powdered rhinoceros horn is regarded as an aphrodisiac.

The Unicorn is a good omen; it indicates happiness, and the enjoyment of times which will be long remembered. It is a sign of nobility of character, and good will. Its appearance is always auspicious, and if in the East indicates a birth. It shows quickness of mind; the scholar Wen Ching lit a unicorn horn and used it as a candle in order to be able to see supernatural creatures in a dark river. Hence, it shows ingenuity. By extension, indicates an invitation from a high-ranking person.

In matters of romance, the Unicorn indicates a happy and lasting relationship. In business, it indicates successful dealings, and amicable relationships. In health, it is a sign of recovery from illness and continuing good health. In the professions, it indicates success in dealing with people, and may refer to public relations. It shows a wealth of ideas, and a career in which one can put ideas to work. It may signify the newer professions in advertising, or the film industry.

Chung tile: There will shortly be an event which you will have occasion to remember with pleasure for many years. Pleasure in company.

First tile: An auspicious sign, especially where personal relationships are concerned. Friends, happiness, joyful events are indicated.

Last tile: The hoof of the unicorn; a symbol of good luck. An unexpected piece of luck; a pleasant surprise.

In the East: The Unicorn in the East signifies friendly relations and pleasant company. It indicates progress, the making of new friends, and pleasant journeys.

In the South: This indicates a short stay away from home with friends, for a happy occasion; it may mean the wedding of a relative to which one is invited.

In the West: Unexpected visitors bring good news. Correspondence bringing good news from abroad. There will be progress.

In the North: An invitation from a high-ranking person. Recognition for services; promotion. If with water, a long journey, travel abroad.

9 Circles-White   NOBILITY   (*See* **White**)

(vii) THE WAN TILES

Like our own word myriad, the word Wan means ten thousand, but also any large number, limitless, or an indefinite period of time. The ancient meaning of the character was 'scorpion' and the stylized outline of a scorpion may be seen in the Chinese character; the two feelers, its segmented body, and the tail with a sting in it.

The Wan tiles are all red and black; all of them are therefore potentially danger signals; there is always the element of the sting in the scorpion's tail causing unexpected harm. The presence of a Wan tile in a group may indicate danger from that quarter, whether from people who were thought to be friends, or the onset of illness, or through accident or carelessness in some other matter. The position of the Wan tile, and its relation to the other tiles in its group, will indicate the time, the manner and the severity of the danger.

There is, fortunately, another side to the meaning of the Wan tiles. Another sign for ten thousand, or Wan, was the fylfot (卍), the sign which was reversed by the Nazis for their swastika emblem. The fylfot means 'the heart of Buddha' and therefore can mean compassion, grace, mercy. It has these attributes in connection with any green tile, such as Fa (Beginning) or the five green Bamboo tiles, two (Duck; three (Toad); four (Carp); six (Water); and eight (Mushrooms).

The Wan tiles generally signify intellectual pursuits. They indicate theorists rather than practical persons; pure science rather than applied science; architects rather than builders; painters and musicians rather than craftsmen. They indicate the making of plans (which can of course be extended to mean the making of plots and scheming), intellectual or literary games and pastimes. The tendency is nevertheless always towards figures rather than letters, which are properly the province of the Bamboo tiles.

1 Wan   ENTERING   (Ju) 入

UNITY — FIRST — BEGINNING — SOURCE OF ALL THINGS — INSPIRATION

Guardian: Plum

With Guardian: A Bow

Secondary meaning: An arrow is shot from a bow and hits the target. There will be successful achievement.

Commentary

The sign — is the first and most basic Chinese character. It therefore refers to anything fundamental. In its positive sense, it can mean precedence over other people, being chosen, and independence. In Chinese writing, when placed above a sign it means Heaven; when below, the Earth. Its positive meanings are revealed when it is in harmony with a green tile, especially if next to 4 Bamboo, Carp, which means success in examinations. Similar interpretations are found with its being in association with Fa, when it takes on its secondary meaning, whether or not with its proper Guardian, of an arrow leaving the bow and hitting the mark. Even with Chung, which has an original meaning of a target, 1 Wan will have the reading 'sure success, achievement, and attainment'.

The negative side of this tile means loneliness and desertion. It can mean the isolation which is brought on by having to make an unpopular decision, or being cut off from relatives and friends as a result of doing what one thinks right. It can mean a strongly independent character that breeds resentment. In matters of the heart, it can mean loneliness. It also signifies a barrier, and as such can mean obstinacy, refusal and hindrance. Projects which are planned will meet with set-backs; business may stagnate owing to a lack of direction. If the enquiry is, for example, concerned with an illness, there is no indication of a quick recovery, but fortunately, none that it will worsen.

With money matters, the indication is to rely on firm and conservative investments, rather than take risks, if it appears with red or black tiles. With green tiles, however, there is an indication of success in initiating new ventures.

Chung tile:	Success will come gradually, do not be impatient. To a leading question — Yes.
First tile:	Success in any new venture. Proceed as planned.
Last tile:	A barrier — do not despair; the barrier will be lifted when everything is in order.
In the East:	Firm foundation, solidarity, firmness of purpose and leadership. Success is indicated for relations with other persons in business, and there are signs pointing to promotion and authority.
In the South:	An approach to an obstacle. The warnings are to prepare against possible hold-ups.
In the West:	—, being at the top, indicates Heaven; the interpretation is protection and insurance. With a green tile, Heaven is watching and protecting. With a black tile, be prepared; beware; take no risks.
In the North:	Hindrances; but also, moving away from a barrier. You may be finding that the barrier to success has already been lifted, or be planning a way round it.

1 Wan-Beginning INITIATION (*see* **Beginning**)
1 Wan-4 Bamboo RECONCILIATION (*see* **4 Bamboo**)

———————————— • ————————————

2 Wan DOUBLE-EDGED SWORD (Chien)

DUALITY — TWINS — A PAIR — BALANCE — EQUILIBRIUM

Guardian:	Spring
With Guardian:	Soldiers
Secondary meaning:	Soldiers indicate a group of people who concentrate their efforts under leadership to attain a common end. Co-operation.

Commentary

The character for 'Double-Edged Sword' is similar to that for the bamboo-slips used in divination. It indicates the ancient use of the two-edged sword in divination, which may account for the many legends of singing and speaking swords, or even the 'Sword of Damocles'.

This sign, although called The Double-Edged Sword, is really more beneficient in aspect than its name might suggest. It has only a negative aspect when in association with certain tiles, namely, the three 'black' Circle tiles, 6, 7 and 8. The meanings of these negative associations are respectively: 6 Circles, jealousy, where two peach trees, or women, are vying for attention; 7 Circles, irritations and quarrels, where two ants vex and annoy the sufferer; and 8 Circles, violent argument, which is the representation of two tigers battling together.

More positive are its aspects with green tiles, where it indicates the good fortune arising from co-operation and partnership. Forming one of the Nine Felicitous Associations with 2 Bamboo (Duck) it there indicates marriage or lifelong companionship. If the question posed relates to business, it would indicate a successful merger. With the Carp (4 Bamboo) instead of indicating quarrels, it means that differences will be solved; with the Toad, it indicates an unusual relationship, or unexpected alliance, for toads are rarely seen together.

Just as 1 Wan indicated Heaven or Earth, so 2 Wan indicates Heaven *and* Earth, since the line — is in both the top and bottom positions, representing balance and equilibrium. It shows the merging together of Yin and Yang, positive with negative, masculine with feminine. It can therefore mean, by extension, completion and perfection. It therefore enhances perfect tiles, indicating the completion and successful fulfilment of whatever venture the perfect tile ruled.

Chung tile:	An announcement of an engagement, merger or partnership. A satisfactory outcome of a disputed point.
First tile:	Success in joint ventures. Co-operation will bring hoped for results.
Last tile:	A division; sharing; delegation. The meaning is not separation, but fission, in order that both parts may more successfully grow.
In the East:	In the reader's place, 2 Wan indicates involvement

in some joint or co-operative venture which is happening at the moment. Balance, equilibrium and harmonious relationships are indicated.

In the South: There is a reference to a partnership which had been dissolved in the past; there is a possibility of its renewal being discussed. The outcome will be shown by other tiles.

In the West: In opposition to the reader, there are signs that outside sources may try to break up an existing partnership. Guard against this.

In the North: 2 Wan in the North is not a good sign, but a warning of a threat or an impending quarrel. A green tile adjacent will indicate a successful outcome, a black one an unfortunate event.

2 Wan, 2 Bamboo COMPANIONSHIP (*see* 2 Bamboo)
Also see the commentary, p.124.

———————————— ● ————————————

3 Wan EARTH (Ti) 地

LAND — GROUND — TERRITORY — LOCALITY — MOTIVE

Guardian: Chrysanthemum

With Guardian: Snake

Secondary meaning: The snake is the symbol of the Earth, and of new life, indicated by the sloughing of its skin. Snakes are able to give forewarning of earthquakes, and leave the crevices in which they normally hide. The snake therefore warns against dangers with Earth and Land.

Commentary
The number 3 is the symbol of Heaven, Earth and Man, represented by

the three lines which form the Chinese character for 3. It is a picture of the first trigram of the I Ching, and as such is known as Ch'ien, which signifies Heaven. But Three may also signify three broken lines; hence the meaning is also that of the eighth Trigram, signifying the earth, K'un. Three is the number of the imperishables; virtue, merit, and what one has taught to others. It is the number of the three things which are not for the asking: wealth, offspring — and a long beard! It is the number of the three worlds: the past, present, and future.

Principally, however, with 3 Wan, the number represents the Earth in its relationship to man. Three o'clock (in a Chinese expression) is taken to mean the three seasons, spring, summer and autumn, which are the farming seasons. In 3 Wan we see the Earth laid out, ploughed in rows. It is the symbol of land, and of estates. It indicates farming, property and journeys by land. It indicates territories, countries, disputes over borders. It is concerned less with Man on the Earth than with what Man does with the Earth. The Earth was, and still is in some sects, the greatest object of veneration. It is, after all, the greatest thing under Heaven. Life springs from the Earth and returns to it. It was the custom of the Emperor to symbolically plough a field every year. Then a clay cow would be broken up, and the pieces scattered over the ground — an obvious relic of ancient sacrificial rites.

The only human symbolism in Earth is motive; for the Earth tile is not concerned with human relationships. The Earth tile asks for reasons, for actions, for deeds, and is more concerned about the fruitful results. Therefore the 3 Wan tile asks for what reason a course of action is being undertaken; what the object is; what the underlying motives really are. In matters of the heart, therefore, the 3 Wan tile does not signify a romantic attachment. It is too concerned with practicalities; it may indicate a marriage of convenience.

In matters of business, the 3 Wan tile is not concerned with personal relationships; it is the result which matters. It asks the questioner to take a hard look at the facts and to forget the frills and his own preferences for particular actions. In matters of health, the Earth tile indicates a robust constitution, and an outdoor-loving personality. It does not hold out false optimism and deals sternly with imaginary invalids. It favours those courses of treatment which emphasize exercise and a healthy diet.

Of the professions, it shows agriculture and estate management as its favoured careers.

Chung tile: The powerful influences indicated by Earth are an
                       indication of intercession on your behalf from some-

one with great authority. Assistance to achieve your aims.

First tile:	The Earth tile in the first place is an indication of great effort; it may mean moving into a bigger concern; or upheaval in moving into the country.
Last tile:	The Earth tile in the last place indicates a reserve of great power. It can also mean loneliness or isolation; projects which cause one to be separated from family.
In the East:	The Earth tile in the East sections shows forces flowing between you, or your affairs and environment, and those in authority. It shows change and movement on a large scale.
In the South:	The Earth in the South indicates great abundance and fertility; it shows great effort, an increase in trade; demands made upon you. Prosperity for the present.
In the West:	There is an indication of movement; plans, and new strategies. It indicates maps and lines. Long distance communications by land; passage of goods.
In the North:	There is an indication of a pioneering spirit: it shows vast expanses of empty land waiting for development. It indicates boundaries being re-formed. There is bleakness, like white paper which has not yet been written upon. Reserves of power.

3 Wan, 6 Bamboo ABUNDANCE   (*See* **6 Bamboo**)

————————————   ●   ————————————

4 Wan LUTE   (Ch'in)

PROPRIETY — ENJOYMENT — CULTURAL PURSUITS — FRIENDS

Guardian: Autumn

With Guardian: Wine

Secondary meaning: Two men sit beneath the trees; one drinks wine and
                     the other plays on the lute.

Commentary

The symbolism of the number 4 is the square, also the four divisions of
Yin and Yang into Greater and Lesser Yin, and Greater and Lesser
Yang. Mathematically, 4 can be expressed as $2+2$, or 2×2. The science
of numbers is wrapped up with the science of music; the correct tuning of
instruments, vital for the sound to be acceptable and aesthetically
satisfying, depends on the exact relationships between the pitches of the
notes. 4 Wan therefore symbolizes Music and Mathematics; intellectual
pursuits; literature; an appreciation of problems as diverting exercises.
The character for 4 shows a resemblance to that for the West, and also to
the character for wine.

4 Wan indicates stillness; leisure; refined company; eventual progress;
a holding back, but not of stagnation. It is an indication of respite,
reconsideration, review.

In matters of the heart, it is a warning not to go rushing into a relationship that has just been made. It is a warning to stand back and appraise
the situation carefully. The same applies to matters of business.

Careers indicated are those involving quiet study; the gentler pursuits;
writing, librarianship. Also, matters to do with figures and accounts are
favoured; all careers which require careful attention to details.

In health matters, 4 Wan indicates recovery after convalescence.

Chung tile: Success in examinations; relaxation and opportun-
                     ities for enjoyment.

First tile: New friends; harmonious relationships; a richer
                     appreciation of the resources available.

Last tile: A warning against impatience; the need to review and look into detail. Overlooked flaws.

In the East: New friends; abstruse questions will be discussed at length. Eventual progress.

In the South: Questions of estate or scientific matters will need to be resolved. Increase in paperwork; the need to work steadily without hurry.

In the West: Gentle progress; slow but sure. Little by little improvements are made. The steps which take longest are those which go furthest.

In the North: A warning against rashness. Matters are not as simple as you would wish them to be. There are additional complications which need to be resolved before embarking on the next step.

4 Wan, 4 Bamboo   RECONCILIATION

———————————— • ————————————

5 Wan   HOUSE   (Fang)

WAITING – SOLIDITY – DEPENDIBILITY – CERTAINTY

Guardian: Autumn

With Guardian: Stone

Secondary meaning: A house built of stone which endures all kinds of ravages.

Commentary

The character for the figure 5 shows Heaven, Mankind, and the Earth together, and the Emperor ruling over the Earth. Five therefore signifies authority. The number 5 (because the Centre is considered to be part of it) is the symbol of the Earth; the five directions. The Earth is square, unlike Heaven, which is a circle. Houses may be made of wood or other materials, but the house represented by 5 Wan is one built of enduring stone. Five also refers to the five elements: earth, water, fire, wood, and metal. The five elements are contained in a house; there is a foundation in earth, wood is used in its construction, and in the house there is a fire on which the metal utensils are set to boil the water.

The house has windows, doors, chimneys, and furniture, and these attributes are secondary symbols of the house. The House is associated with home and family. In the East it signifies returning home, family attachments. In the West, it indicates moving away from home. In the North and South it indicates business, especially in construction, or in the buying and selling of real estate. In matters of romance, it is an indication of marriage, settling down and starting a large family. In matters of health, it signifies a short stay in hospital, and returning home. It warns against accidents in the home; against danger from fire. It also indicates family quarrels, but that there is no danger from these. With any 8 tile it signifies a happy household.

Chung tile:	The Chung tile, a stone, indicates that there will be little alteration from the present position. It signifies waiting.
First tile:	The House as the first tile signifies happy family relationships and family reunions. It signifies marriage and many children.
Last tile:	In the last position, the House indicates little change from present business prospects; it indicates solidity and reliability, and applies to old-established firms with a sound reputation.
In the East:	In the East, the House shows happy family relationships. It also shows alterations and improvements to the home; the possibilities of extending and improving the house.
In the South:	The House indicates business dealings within a small but relied circle. It may indicate changes within the firm itself which will lead to promotion. It indicates a strengthening of position.
In the West:	The House indicates a possibility of removal; the

home is shown far away. Alternatively, it could mean a long journey for the whole family.

In the North: The indications are for projects and investments to be soundly based. There is no indication of change; it is best to wait before implementing any new plans.

5 Wan, 8 Bamboo KNOWLEDGE   (*See* **8 Bamboo**)

———————————————   •   ———————————————

6 Wan FIRE   (Huo) 火

ACTION — LEADERSHIP — ENERGY — DRIVE

Guardian: Chrysanthemum

With Guardian: Ting (Ritual Cauldron)

Secondary meaning: Food prepared as for a sacrificial offering; the will of Heaven is fulfilled; progress, and success.

Commentary

The element fire is a sign of progress, movement and vitality. It signifies action, speed, and the energy and impatience with which changes are brought about. It shows dissatisfaction with the present and a desire to make a new start in spite of opposition. Fire is one of the five elements; it consumes wood, and is quenched by water. Hence, with the Tree tiles it shows even greater change, not necessarily for the best. It would signify the upsetting of established principles; it could mean changes that would not be for personal benefit. The go-ahead qualities of fire are dampened by water and watery tiles; it could indicate that far-reaching plans would not come to fruition.

   The Guardian of the Fire tile is the Chrysanthemum, which is the emblem of the sun, because of its resemblance to its rays. The chrysanthemum is associated with Imperial power, and hence, the Fire tile can mean movement into higher social circles. The Ting is a three-legged cauldron which was placed in the fire to cook ceremonial meats as part of the old rituals. It is therefore a sacred and revered object; it indicates that duties have been performed satisfactorily and that there will be recognition. The association with autumn is very strong; the Chinese character for autumn shows the characters for wood and fire side by side: it represents the fields being burnt after the harvests. The Fire tile therefore may mean, symbolically, change and progress in the autumn.

The doubled Fire tile, in the same sector, indicates fireside conversation, but two Fire tiles in opposite sectors indicates danger.

Figuratively, the word fire is used to mean rage, lust, and uncontrolled emotions. The dangers of fire are shown in the common expressions 'touch-paper', 'rocket', 'blazing' and so on, expressions which are common to all languages. The Fire tile therefore indicates undue emotional upheaval.

Because of the various interpretations of the Fire tile, it should be taken in regard to the tiles around it, bearing in mind its tendency to destroy the aspect of 'wood' or the 'Tree' tiles.

6 Wan and 6 Bamboo in opposite sectors (North-South or East-West) indicates calamity or disaster on a large scale.

6 Wan indicates energy in other forms; it may refer to electrical energy, nuclear power, or chemical energy.

In matters of romance, the Fire tile indicates a passionate relationship from which no good will result. Regarding personal relationships as a whole, it shows erratic and violent behaviour leading to the breaking up of friendships.

In business, it signifies sudden action and commotion; the flaring up of some new emergency which has to be taken care of immediately.

In health matters, it indicates treatment by the most modern technical methods; it shows illnesses to be of short duration.

In matters of a career, it indicates the sciences.

Generally speaking, Fire indicates a tendency to rashness, and is a warning to proceed with caution.

Chung tile: The Fire tile indicates powerful forces which can be used for good or bad. It may indicate a new and influential friend; one should proceed with caution and ensure one is not being used. New plans may quickly die out.

First tile: The first tile indicates a sudden burst of energy or compulsive actions. Benefits can only be short term.

Last tile: Fire in the last place indicates grave danger. If associated with one of the Three Trees, it signifies the loss of something valuable.

In the East:	In the East, Fire may be employed to its best advantage; it shows considerable energy which can be employed for successful ends. It is an indication of immediate resources which have to be harnessed at once.
In the South:	The indications are of a sudden stroke of luck; it may be in the form of a new contract, or a friend who has offered his services. Best use must be made at once if the full scope of advantage is to be taken.
In the West:	Fire in the West indicates the scrapping of old-established customs; getting rid of 'dead wood'. It may be necessary to make sacrifices to adapt to the new methods.
In the North:	An indication of danger; the more so if in association with any of the Tree tiles; eventual recovery is shown by 'moist' tiles in association.

6 Wan, 6 Bamboo   PROGRESS   (*See* **6 Bamboo**)

———————————— • ————————————

7 Wan   SEVEN STARS   (Tou) 斗

GOVERNMENT — JUDGEMENT — LAW — EDICTS

Guardian: Orchid

With Guardian: A chess-piece; the Pole Star

Secondary meaning: Scattered like the stars across the sky, or like the pieces on a chess board, yet the Pole Star remains constant and immutable. Certainty in the midst of confusion.

Commentary

Chinese literature makes frequent parallels between the stars in the Heavens and the pieces on a chess board. Even the term 'Hsiang', meaning elephant, and which is also used to mean the judgements of the I Ching (see the Introduction), is used figuratively to mean the stars. The 7 Wan tile refers to the seven stars which make up the 'Dipper' of the Great Bear. It revolves in the sky, pointing out the position of the Pole Star. The Pole Star, centre of Heaven, was regarded as the apotheosis of the Emperor. In earthly life, the Emperor stood at the Centre of the Earth, and the whole of the known Universe revolved round the Emperor's commands. Thus the Seven Stars represent judgements; laws, decisions which cannot be altered. They also represent universal, scientific laws: the world of the mathematician and physicist.

Yet the significance is not confined to bare algebraic formulae; it indicates creative thought; for physical and mathematical laws are able to generate new concepts and new terms. It is in the skilful application of these laws that new discoveries are made. The Seven Stars therefore indicate creative thinking and research.

In matters of the heart, 7 Wan does not indicate 'romance under the stars' in the popular sense of the word; it indicates attachments that go deeper than mere passing fancies; relationships which are the marriage of two minds.

In business matters, there are indications of litigation; it is necessary to be scrupulous in attention to legal details.

In matters of health, it indicates a course of treatment which will be undertaken while the patient is still leading a full life — regular check-ups; out-patient treatment, and so on.

Careers indicated are those concerned with physics, mathematics, navigation, pure research, and similar fields.

Chung tile:	There will be success in attempts to improve matters for other people; realization of plans which have altruistic motives. Vicarious pleasure.
First tile:	A spark; a decision in your favour. Rejoicing. Studies; a judgement that will need careful consideration; a complex contract. Be wary.
Last tile:	The star on the horizon. Hope. A signal. An indication of the route to take.
In the East:	The rising sun obscures the stars; judgement will be clouded. Be punctilious.
In the South:	The influence of the stars is totally lost in the Southern sector. The adjoining tiles take precedence.

In the West: The Stars begin to show their influence: it indicates insight, a clearer appreciation of detail. There is an ability to review things more carefully now that distractions have been removed.

In the North: The Stars at their maximum influence. Benignity or stern judgements are dependent on the associated tiles.

7 Wan, 4 Bamboo   REWARD   (*See* 4 Bamboo)

——————————————   •   ——————————————

8 Wan   A KNOT   (Chieh) 結

UNITING – UNWINDING – CONGEALING – UNRAVELLING

Guardian: Winter

With Guardian: Silk Thread

Secondary meaning: A young maiden winds silk on to a bobbin.

Commentary

One of the most difficult tiles to interpret, 8 Wan indicates confusion; it also indicates the unravelling of confusion. The silk is wound on a bobbin; it is woven into cloth. Similarly, the thin thread of the spider is woven into a mesh to trap the unwary. The character for 8 signifies cutting; therefore, it signifies the cutting of the knot. Furthermore, in the China of archaic times, even before there was oracle bone writing, messages were sent by complex patterns of knots in cords.

The significance of 8 Wan is: confusion and disorder, either being unravelled with patience, or cut through at a stroke. Compulsive repetition; impulsive action.

An alternative reading of this sign is a bond or contract; as an answer to a specific question, therefore 8 Wan signifies the binding together of two parties; but where another 8 appears, it means the severance of an existing contract. The binding, congealing, uniting aspects of Chieh is shown by odd-numbered tiles; the severing, separating aspect is shown by even-numbered tiles. It follows that the interpretations of 8 Wan have to be taken in the light of associated tiles.

In matters of romance, 8 Wan signifies the tying or untying of a knot; it indicates marriage or the breaking off of an engagement. It does not indicate flirtatious or shallow encounters.

In business, it shows the forming, or breaking, of partnerships. It does not show protracted litigation.

In matters of health it indicates complications during the development of an illness, and patient regard to the unravelling of the complexities of its progress.

Of the trades and professions, the Knot indicates textiles and fashion.

Chung tile:	The unravelling of complexities; a solution to problems. Eventual solution; perhaps unexpectedly.
First tile:	Confusion rules; there are too many issues at stake; it is necessary to sort out matters one at a time; nothing will be achieved by trying to do too much at once.
Last tile:	If problems persist, it may be best to cut through them at a stroke. Nothing will be gained by present exertions in all directions.
In the East:	Spiders begin to weave their webs in the morning; already the net has been cast. Well and good if you are the spider. Elaborate plans.
In the South:	Diligence; attention to detail; contracts being drawn up.
In the West:	There is need to cut through a forest of weeds which is beginning to engulf the garden. 'Unable to see the wood for the trees'; a re-appraisal.
In the North:	There is either a severing of links, or the dissolving of partnerships indicated; otherwise matters in general will become burdensome.

8 Wan, 3 Bamboo DISCOVERY   **(See 3 Bamboo)**

9 Wan HEAVEN (T'ien)

HONOUR — FULFILMENT — SPIRITUALITY — SUPREME JOY

Guardian: Spring

With Guardian: Rebirth

Secondary meaning: The fate of the myriad people is governed by the Queen Mother of the West; only kings, sages and holy men are controlled by the Nine Lords of Heaven.

Commentary

The words of Lao Tzu, which appear as the Secondary Meaning above, are certainly open to considerable interpretation, and would no doubt find fierce opposition to the point of view as it stands. The Nine Lords of Heaven, here signified by the 9 of 9 Wan, control the fates and destinies of those who submit themselves to Heaven's will. The 'myriad' people (the masses, as the expression goes today) are less concerned with spiritual matters; they are therefore ruled by showy splendour; their interest is attracted by the Queen Mother of the West, in her magnificent tiara (in which she is always portrayed), her dazzling purple gowns, and her attendant blue birds. Those in positions of power, and the wealthy, are not impressed by ostentatious display; those who are wiser, the sages, do not envy shows of extravagance; holy men do not even bother to contemplate earthly things, for their sights are already fixed higher. This is why it is said that the 'myriad' (the meaning of Wan) people are not under the rule of Heaven. Wealth and riches do not come to everyone; wisdom, or quick-wittedness, is not given to everyone at birth; we may strive to achieve both of these things and fail. But the precepts of Heaven, and the correct path, are there for all who would use them. The guidance of Heaven is open to all who would seek it; the 9 Wan tile, the twenty-seventh of the suit tiles, and the final tile of all, signifies the one person out of the myriad people with whom the Nine Lords may concern themselves when they have finished writing the destinies of kings and scholars.

Heaven means both the spiritual Heaven of the scriptures and the heavens in the sense of the sky or the Universe. It can mean natural (as opposed to artificial), especially when in conjunction with 2 Wan or 3 Wan. It means 'the Heavens' in the astronomical sense when joined with 7 Wan. In the sense of 'day' it can mean daytime, or a short period of time — i.e., in a matter of days.

It takes on a fuller spiritual sense when it appears with White: in this sense it means purity, spiritual grace, and religion. It is the abode of the souls of the dead, and White is the colour of the soul. It indicates disenchantment with material things; disillusionment, but the finding of inner peace.

The less spiritual, the more materialistic, those who are ruled by 'the Queen Mother of the West', will take satisfaction in knowing that 9 Wan also signifies air travel. It reveals honours, fulfilment, and gains, particularly if it appears in the West sector, or with West tile.

In matters of the heart, it indicates spiritual love and resignation to one's fate.

In business matters it is certainly a good sign, especially for the ruthless and uncaring. Their rewards will be on the earth, not in Heaven. For business deals, it shows satisfaction within days.

In matters of health, it indicates resignation to the course of the illness, whether it will cure itself or not.

Of careers and professions, it suggests that the subject has considered the religious life.

Heaven indicates finality; an end to misfortune. It indicates fulfilment.

Chung tile: There is a sign of approval; your task will be completed and your efforts will be recognized.

First tile: That which you are now attempting will achieve success. Be correct and conscientious in your dealings, and your attention to detail will not go unnoticed.

Last tile: Completion. The task which is underway will be finished. There is recognition and reward.

In the East: Success; a feeling of achievement through enjoyment in one's work. Friendly relationships; recognition and approval.

In the South: Fulfilment through actions. Joy in simple things;

disaffection with material possessions. Satisfaction in simpler pursuits. Popularity.

In the West: Material gains; rewards; successes; promotion; achievement. You will get what you have been striving for, but it will not give you the satisfaction you had hoped.

In the North: A task drawing to a close; the sense of achievement; work completed. Regeneration. The completion of one project, and the prospect of another. Renewal of the cycle. The darkest hour heralding the dawn.

5.

PREPARING THE TILES
FOR A READING

The following pages outline two different methods of preparing the tiles for a reading: one comparatively straightforward, the other couched in somewhat elaborate ceremony. The reader will most likely choose the former, and consider that in the second, The Great Method, the amount of preparation is disproportionate to the object of the operation.

Yet considering the elaborate formalities with which the Chinese are able to clothe the most elementary of undertakings, the Great Method, stripped of prayers, incense, and sacrificial offerings to the Eight Spirits, remains a relatively simple ritual. Time should be the last consideration.

The best advised course of action is for the reader to try a few sample readings of 'single-tile' turnings; then to progress to the Little Method. When the reader has acquired confidence and fluency with the tiles and their symbolism, it is time to invite one or two friends to participate in a reading by the Great Method. For those who find even the Little Method time consuming; there is an abbreviated mode of selecting a single tile for a direct answer to a question. This is described in the opening paragraph of Chapter 3.

(i) Casting the Tiles by the Little Method

The tiles are cast, face downwards, on to a table not much less than a yard in diameter. With the right hand, the tiles are then swirled round in an anti-clockwise direction until the reader is satisfied that the tiles are well shuffled. This stage is identical to the first part — 'The Twittering of the Sparrows' — of the Great Method.

Still swirling the tiles in an anti-clockwise direction, make a space in the middle of the tiles by swirling the tiles to the edge. When a suitably large space has been cleared, about half a yard across, and still moving the hand in an anti-clockwise direction, draw thirteen tiles into the middle of the space. These will be caught up by the hand as it moves around the central space. When thirteen tiles have been drawn into the middle, and counted to ensure there are thirteen, the thirteen tiles are given a further swirling called 'Rustling of the Hemp Leaves'.

Next, the three tiles which are furthest away from the reader are separated from the group by being pushed further away. The three tiles furthest to the right are then pushed further to the right; the three furthest to the left even further to the left, and finally the nearest three are drawn nearer to the reader. This will leave one tile in the middle.

There are now four groups of three tiles with one tile in the centre. The group nearest to the reader are in the East, while those furthest away are in the West. Those to his right are in the South, and those to his left in the North. The one in the middle is in the Centre and is known as the Chung (Centre) tile.

Arrange each group of three tiles in a row. Turn the Chung (Centre) tile face upwards. If it is the tile known as Chung (marked with the Chinese symbol (中) in red) it is called The First Blessing. Now turn up the tile which is the left-hand tile of the row nearest the reader (the East row). If the tile is Fa (written (發) in green), it is the second of the Blessings. Next turn up the tile which is the right-hand tile of the row to the left of the reader (the North row). This is called the Last tile, and if it is the White tile it is the third of the Blessings. Finally, turn up all the tiles, beginning with the East, and passing through the other rows in an anti-clockwise direction.

Concerning the Guardians

Should any tile of the thirteen turned up be a Guardian, an extra tile is taken for each Guardian. In the Little Method only extra tiles for the Guardians are taken more or less at random, but generally speaking from the outside circle, nearest to the Guardian. (In the Great Method a more detailed approach is undertaken.)

The extra tile is put in the place of the Guardian, and the Guardian tile is placed on the table immediately above the replacing tile.

Double Tiles

Once all the tiles are placed into the four groups, with the thirteenth tile in the middle, they are examined to see whether they form associations. Firstly, if any group contains a pair of tiles that are exactly the same, these two tiles are placed next to each other and called a *double tile*.

Double tiles can only form associations with other tiles when they are perfect. Thus, two Tortoise tiles (7 Bamboo) which are perfect may form an association with West (a pure black tile), giving a double 'Tortoise in its Own Realm'. Two West tiles may not, however, form an association with the Tortoise tile, nor may one of the West tiles be regarded as doing so. The order is, double tiles first, then associations. In the latter case, the West tiles would retain their own identity, and the Tortoise would retain its own identity and interpretation. The interpretation of the 'Tortoise in its Own Realm' would not apply in this case.

Guardians with Double Tiles and Associations
When a Guardian is replaced by a tile which is part of a double, the Guardian rules the double tile jointly. When a Guardian is replaced by a tile which then forms one of the Nine Felicitous, or Five Harmonious, or Four Three-Tile Associations, or the Four Fabulous Beasts in Their Realms, the Guardian is held to be ruling both the tile and the resultant association, but not the other tiles in the associations.

Summary of the Above Points
Double tiles are paired before associations.

Only perfect double tiles may form associations.

A Guardian rules a double tile jointly.

A Guardian rules its own tile in an association, which keeps its original interpretation. (Without the Guardian it would lose its own interpretation in making the association.) The Guardian does not rule the other tiles of the association individually.

A Guardian also rules the joint association of its tile with another.

(ii) The Great Method of Casting the Tiles
The preparation of the tiles for their divinatory reading by the Great Method of Casting the Tiles is couched in a rather elaborate ceremony, the mystique of which is to prepare the reader's mind for the serious undertaking of interpreting the oracle. When expert players get together for a game of Mah Jongg they shuffle the tiles together, build up the wall, and distribute the tiles among themselves in a few moments. Such haste is neither necessary nor desirable when preparing the tiles for a divinatory reading. The five steps should be undertaken with dignity,

propriety and solemnity of purpose, and the task approached with respect and seriousness. A casual attitude will result in a casual translation, which will be of little value to the person who is consulting the oracle.

The Five Steps
Five Steps have been mentioned as being the procedure for the casting of the tiles. The Five Steps are:

      I The Twittering of the Sparrows
     II The Building of the City
   III The Opening of the Gates
  IV The Rustling of the Leaves
   V The Unfolding of the Books

  By using the Great Method of casting the tiles, it is possible for the reader to consult the oracle on his own behalf as well as that of up to three other persons. (Those that are consulting the oracle will be referred to as *sitters*; one of them will be the *Interpreter* of the tiles for all the sitters, including himself. This sitter is the *Reader*.) The Five Steps followed when consulting the Mah Jongg tiles by the Great Method are now described in detail.

The Twittering of the Sparrows
The Reader and any other sitters, not more than four persons altogether, approach the table and seat themselves around it. If there is only one other sitter besides the Reader, they should face each other. The table should be not much smaller than about a yard across, otherwise there is really not sufficient room to enable the tiles to be adequately handled.

  The tiles are cast on the surface of the table, face downwards. The reader then announces 'The Twittering of the Sparrows' and each person swirls the tiles around with both hands in an anti-clockwise direction until they are thoroughly shuffled to everyone's satisfaction. The reader then announces:

The Building of the City
Four walls are now built; if there are four sitters each person may build a wall in front of him; otherwise the Reader must build up any walls where there is no sitter. The walls are to be built of thirty-six tiles, the tiles being placed with their long sides adjacent to each other. This is done by

taking three tiles in each hand and bringing them together to make a short wall of six tiles; another three tiles are taken in each hand and added to the ends of the row already made; then for a third time three tiles are taken in each hand and added to the row already made. A second row is then built in the same manner, the second row being placed on top of the first row. Thus a wall is built, eighteen tiles long and two tiles deep.

Next with a rod or rack the length of the wall, the walls are pushed together to make a square, their corners touching. It is considered to be of ill-portent if there is a gap between the walls. Mah Jongg players call this 'Keeping the Devil Out'.

The Opening of the Gates

Four dice are now needed. These are normally provided with Chinese Mah Jongg sets and usually have a large red spot in place of the black spot which appears on Western dice. (Obviously, if four dice are not available, one dice must be rolled four times.)

The Reader casts the dice on to the table between the four walls. If 'one' does not show on any of the dice, the dice are rolled again until one or more dice show 'one'.

The number of 'ones' which appears indicates how many Gates which are to be made in each wall. If only one Gate is shown, the procedure is as follows:

The reader announces 'The Opening of the Gates'.

The Reader takes, between the thumb and first and second fingers, four tiles from the middle of the wall on his right, and places them, face down, on the table in front of him, but *outside* the walls. (If, however, the Reader is consulting the oracle on his own behalf only, and there are no other sitters, he places the tiles directly into the centre of the table, *between* the walls.) The Reader then, in a similar manner, takes four tiles from the wall opposite, four tiles from the row on his left, and puts these with the others.

The Reader then takes two tiles from his own wall, between his thumb and forefinger, and places the lower tile on the tile immediately to the right of the gap which appears. The top tile is placed on the table with the other twelve tiles. The stack of three tiles to the right of the gap is called the *Tower*.

If there is a sitter to the right of the Reader, the sitter proceeds in a similar fashion, with slight variations. The sitter picks up four tiles from the middle of the wall on his right. These may be taken from *either side of the Gate*. Four more tiles are similarly drawn from the wall opposite;

again these may be from either side of the Gate. But from the wall of the Reader, he may not take any tiles which include the Tower; the sitter can only take those four tiles at the side of the Gate opposite to the Tower. From his own wall the sitter takes the two tiles at the right hand side of the Gate, placing the lower one on the tiles immediately to the right of the Gate to make his own Tower, and placing the second tile with the twelve he has previously taken.

The other two sitters draw their tiles in a similar way; if there is no Tower, four tiles may be drawn from either side of the Gate. If there is a Tower, the tiles can only be drawn from the side of the Gate opposite the Tower.

There will now be one Gate open in each wall, irrespective of the number of sitters. There will be as many Towers as there are sitters, in the wall facing the sitter, and on the right hand side of the Gate.

Procedure of Opening the Gates, when more than one gate is to
be opened in each wall
As has been previously described, the number of Gates to be opened depends on the number of ones shown by the throwing of the dice.

If Two Gates are to be Opened
The Reader begins to draw tiles from the walls as before, but instead of drawing out a block of four tiles, he draws two tiles, one above the other, from the wall on his right, then the wall opposite, and next the wall on his left. He draws no tiles from his own wall, but goes again to the wall on his right, drawing two more tiles from that wall, thus making a second gap, or Gate. He takes two more from opposite and left walls in a similar way. He draws from his own wall, and builds a Tower, as if there were only one Gate in his own wall.

The sitter on his right may now draw tiles, two at a time, from either side of the two Gates of the walls on his right and opposite. When he comes to the Reader's wall, however, he draws two tiles from that wall, thus making a second Gate. He then draws two further tiles from each wall, again having the opportunity to draw from either side of both Gates. Two tiles at least, however, must be left as a Pillar between the two gates. The tiles forming Pillars between Gates must never be drawn, or the Gates will collapse. He now has to build his Tower, which, as before, is built to the right of the Gate on his right.

The other sitters proceed similarly, drawing from either side of the two Gates, two tiles at a time. Tiles may not be drawn from the Tower side of Gates, nor may tiles be drawn if they are the only two tiles forming a Pillar, as explained above.

When Three Gates are to be Opened
If the dice show three 'ones', and three Gates have to be opened, the modification of opening the gates is that no sitter draws tiles from the wall opposite him, only from the walls to his right and left. The Reader then commences by drawing two tiles from the wall on his right, a further two from the wall on his left. This is repeated three times, so that the walls on his left and right have three Gates, but the wall opposite him remains intact. He then draws his thirteenth tile and builds his Tower as before.

The other sitters follow suit, bearing in mind not to take down any Pillar separating Gates, or drawing from the Tower side of a Gate.

When Four Gates are to be Opened
In the extremely rare cases when four Gates are to be opened, a sitter draws all the tiles from his own wall. In such a case, the sitters may draw their tiles simultaneously. Each sitter draws three stacks of four tiles between the thumb and the first two fingers, ensuring that a Pillar is left between the Gates. The stacks are taken from the wall moving from left to right. Then, at the right hand part of the wall, the sitter draws two tiles, as before, placing the lowest tile on the tile at the side of the Gate, and putting the top tile together with the twelve already drawn.

When each sitter has drawn thirteen tiles, and placed a fourteenth at the side of his right hand gate to make a Tower, the Reader may announce 'The Rustling of the Hemp Leaves'.

An Alternative Manner of Opening the Gates
Some readers may prefer to use an alternative manner of opening the Gates using the bones, Ch'ou (羣) that are often provided with Mah Jongg sets. Many may feel that there is a more authentic touch about these than the perhaps more occidental dice. Both, are however, of ancient origins, as has been explained in Part One.

The purpose of the bones in the Mah Jongg game is a form of tally; a value is decided on for the differently marked bones and these are distributed among the players as 'chips' as at the roulette tables. They are usually marked with one red spot; eight green (or black) spots; five spots, and nine spots.

Take up four bones marked with one red spot, and twenty bones marked with black spots. These are divided equally, two one-spots and ten eight-spots, and grasped in each hand. They are then thrown on to the table between the walls. There is a particular gesture which is observed in doing this; the bones in the left hand are held horizontally, as if grasping a rail in front, while the ones in the right hand are held perpendicularly to them, as if one were pulling a rope. They are all thrown together; holding the two sets of bones at an angle in the manner described ensures that they are thoroughly shuffled in their descent.

Now examine the bones. Most of them will be bunched together in the centre, but some will have separated. See how many 'ones' are separated from the rest. The number of 'ones' indicates the number of Gates to be made in each wall, in the manner already described.

(Note: obviously, if there are no separate ones, the bones are picked up and thrown again.)

The Rustling of the Hemp Leaves

The Reader may wish to consult the oracle on his own behalf, or not, as the case may be. If he personally wishes to consult the oracle, and there are other sitters, he may consult on his own behalf before or after the other sitters have had their tiles read, according to the Reader's wishes. The Reader will read the tiles of each sitter, and the procedure is exactly the same for himself as the others. The sitters are taken in order, beginning with the sitter on the reader's right.

The sitter transfers all his tiles, still face downwards, to the middle of the table between the walls. The sitter whirls the tiles round in an anti-clockwise direction.

It is the Reader who divides the tiles into their Five Cardinal Groups. The three furthest away from him are pushed away, as in the Little Method. Then the three furthest to his right are pushed more to the right; those three furthest to his left further to his left, and the three nearest to him he draws towards him, leaving one in the centre.

The Four Directions

It has already been mentioned that in Chinese Philosophy there were said to be Five Cardinal Points, namely, East, South, West, North and Centre. The tiles have now been distributed to these Five Cardinal Points. Those nearest to the reader are in the East, those to his right in the South, those furthest away to the West, and those on his left in the North. The tile remaining in the middle is of course the Central Cardinal Point.

The central tile is turned over. If it is Chung (Centre) it is a Blessing.

The first of the three East tiles is turned over; that is to say, the tile on the left of the three. If it is a Fa (Beginning) it is a Blessing. The other tiles are now turned over, moving round in anti-clockwise order. If the last tile turned over (that is, the third of the North tiles) is Pai (White), it is a Blessing.

The Three Blessings are of good omen, and presage well; fortune, escape from danger, and felicity.

The Opening of the Books

The tiles are arranged into their respective associations of doubles and other associations. This is explained fully at the end of the section on the Little Method (p. 179). There is no difference in allocating the doubles and associations, but an important difference between the Little and Great Methods with regards to drawing extra tiles for the Guardians.

Drawing Tiles for the Guardians by the Great Method

As with the Little Method, any Guardians that appear are replaced by tiles over which the Guardians rule, together with any doubles or associations that are formed.

The extra tile is taken from the top of the sitter's Tower. If there are more than one Guardian the Reader will move round the tiles in an anticlockwise direction, replacing the tiles from the Tower. It is possible that a second Guardian may be drawn in its place. It too will guard whatever tile is subsequently drawn, which will have greater significance in the reading. Should it so happen that all three tiles are taken from the Tower, and a fourth has to be drawn, the next tiles to the Tower are taken as necessary.

The Reader will then announce the 'Opening of the Books' for that sitter, and read the tiles according to the interpretations which are given in the preceding pages. When the tiles have been read, the tiles are removed from the table. The Reader then announces 'The Rustling of the Hemp Leaves' for the next sitter, and the same procedure as before is followed.

Concluding the Readings

When the last sitter's tiles have been read, the Reader takes the tile from the Centre (if there was originally a Guardian tile in the Centre, the Reader takes the tile which *replaced* the Guardian) and raps it sharply on the table three times, announcing, 'The Books are Closed' (or if it is preferred, 'The Leaves have ceased their rustling, and the sparrows are all silent').

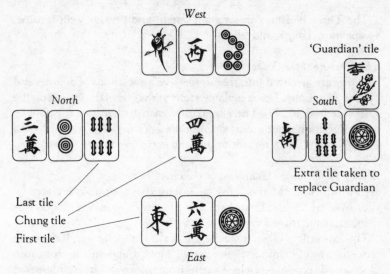

The tiles are (reading from left to right in each case): *East*: East, 6 Wan, 1 Circle; *South*: South, 7 Bamboo; 1 Circle; *West*: 1 Bamboo, West, 7 Circles; *North*: 3 Wan, 2 Circles, 6 Bamboo. The Chung (central) tile is 4 Wan.

MAH JONGG TILES SET OUT FOR DIVINATION

(iii) A Specimen Interpretation of the Tiles

This interpretation refers to the spread of tiles shown above. The Reader is at the stage where the First, Last and Chung tiles have been noted, but they have not yet been put into any Associations. Because one of the tiles turned up was a Guardian, an extra tile has been taken from the remaining tiles. The Guardian indicates that if the 1 Circle tile in South is associated with any other tile in that group of three, it will still retain its own identity.

(As it happens, there are no associations in the South group, nor is Plum the proper guardian of 1 Circle; the tiles therefore retain their own identity.)

First, it is necessary to look through the tiles for any Associations. Beginning in the East, we see that there is a 6 Bamboo in the North, which would make an Association with the 6 Wan if they were in the same triad; but as they are not in the same sector, this does not count. Similarly, neither the 1 Circle of East, nor the 1 Circle of South, can make an Association with the 1 Bamboo in the West. For the same reason, the two 1 Circle tiles do not count as a double tile. Looking at each piece in turn, however, and comparing them with the Index to the

Catalogue of Tiles (p. 73), we see that in the North sector, there is an Association: 3 Wan and 6 Bamboo, which form the Association 'Abundance'. Accordingly, these two tiles are put together as a pair and treated as one tile.

We are now ready to begin the interpretation of the tiles.

The first thing to notice is the 1 Circle in both the East and South sectors: this indicates a continuation of the 1 Circle aspect. The other thing which immediately strikes the attention is the presence of three Cardinal Points, and that each of them is in its own sector. This is a very fortunate sign indeed, showing powerful forces at work. The next step is to study the readings of the tiles. As this is a hypothetical case, it will be necessary to invent a 'sitter' and imagine that he is asking general advice about business and career prospects — plus, of course, any additional information that might come his way.

The Chung tile, 4 Wan, shows relaxation and opportunities for enjoyment. The first tile is East, signifying the questioner being master of the situation, and making pertinent decisions. The last tile (no longer in the same place, since it has been moved to make the association) indicates turmoil — an indication of conflict, upheaval and the unexpected.

In the East, generally associated with the questioner's immediate problems, his character, and environment, we find East itself, together with the Pearl, and Fire. All three of these tiles suggest improvements for the sitter's business prospects; the East showing the questioner's mastery of the situation, Pearl showing the signing of a contract, and Fire suggesting energy which can be used for immediate ends. Continuing from the present into the near future, we see that Pearl (the contract) is still in operation. It is aided by South in its own sector which here indicates a long journey 'for business or pleasure'. The Tortoise in the South indicates worldwide communications, but adds the rider that matters may not be as simple as the questioner would like them to be.

Turning to the West, we see more indications of travel, and warnings. There is a warning against self-indulgence (Peacock in the West) and dwindling resources (West in the West). The Insect also warns against letting attention to duties slacken. This is entirely in agreement with Fire in the East, which is a sign of sudden, but temporary prosperity. The indications are a clear warning to the questioner to take particular care once he has made his initial business contacts.

Finally, we turn to the North, and see what the significance of the Association between the 3 Wan and 6 Bamboo tiles produces. It reads: 'Water and Earth together make clay . . . development of projects . . . return for investment'.

Summing up, the trends indicated by this spread of Mah Jongg tiles shows the signing of a new contract which will lead to the expansion of business and the possibility of developing overseas trade, or certainly travel abroad. Opportunities will arise for 'relaxation and enjoyment' but the danger is over-indulgence in these leisure pursuits. By keeping a careful hold on matters, and a tight rein on expenditure during a tempting period of growth, the final outcome will prove extremely fortunate.

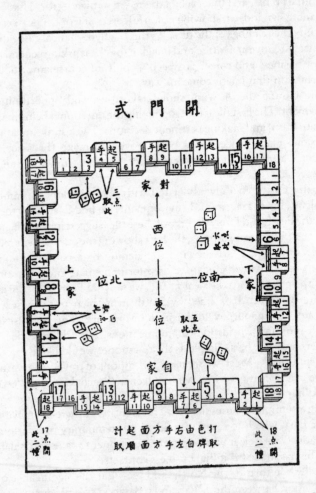

An illustration from a Chinese manual on Mah Jongg (Hsin Ch'ang Ma Ch'üeh P'ai Ta Ch'üan) showing 'The Opening of the Gates' (see pp. 181-184).

SELECT BIBLIOGRAPHY

Needham, J. and Wang Ling. *Science and Civilization in China*, Cambridge (particularly volumes 2, 3 and 4).

Anonymous/Pseudonymous

Directions of Playing Mah Jong 'Chinese Game of Four Winds'.

Hsin Ch'ang Ma Ch'üeh P'ai Ta Ch'üan (The New Edition of the Complete Mah Jongg).

Ku Pen Chu Chiai Huang Ta Shen Ling Ch'ien (The Book of Indications of the Great Yellow Genie).

Kuan Sheng Ti Ling Ch'ien (The Book of Indications of the Ruler of the Sacred Barrier).

Bary, W. T. and Embree, A. T., *Guide to the Oriental Classics*.

Carus, P., *Chinese Astrology. Open Court.* (Available in a modern, but abridged, reprint. Very little about Chinese Astrology itself, but contains useful background information.)

Chatley, H., 'Chinese Natural Philosophy and Magic', *Journal of the Royal Society of Arts*, Vol. LIX, 1911.

Culin, S., *Religious Ceremonies in China*, Privately printed, 1877.

Report of the US National Museum, 1893, 1896.

Chinese Games with Dice and Dominoes, 1893.

Doolittle, J., *Handbook of the Chinese language*, 1872.

Eitel, E. J., *Feng Shui*, Trubner 1873. Reprinted in 1973, 1979.

Gascoigne, B., *Treasures and Dynasties of China*, Cape.

Hedley, G. and Seeley, Y., *Know the Game — Mah Jong*, E.P.

Hsü Ch'in T'ing., *I Ching Yen Chiu* (I Ching Researches), Wu Chow.

Hughes, E. R., *Chinese Philosophy in Classical Times*, Dent.

Kotewall, R. and Smith, N. L., *The Penguin Book of Chinese Verse*, Penguin.

Loewe, M., *Ancient Cosmologies*, Allen and Unwin.
Ways to Paradise, Allen and Unwin.
Everyday Life in Early Imperial China, Batsford.

Lu Hsun., *Brief History of Chinese Fiction*, Foreign Language Press, Pekin.

Mayers, W. F., *Chinese Readers' Manual*, Presbyterian Press, Shanghai 1874.

*Millington, A. D., *The Complete Book of Mah-Jongg*, Barker.

*Robertson, M., *The Game of Mah Jong*.

Schafer, E. H., *Ancient China*, Time Life.

Tsao Hsueh Ch'in, *A Dream of Red Mansions*.

Wilkinson, Sir Wm. H., *The Game of Khanhoo*, 1875.

* Smiths have not got them listed on Compute

INDEX TO PART ONE